In this gorgeous book, Anjum Anand reveals the simple way to serve up the delicious flavours of India at home... fast. Here are more than 100 new quick and easy Indian-inspired recipes, for vegetarians, pescatarians and omnivores alike. Choose to eat 30 minutes after walking into the kitchen, or spend just minutes on a dish that is left to cook itself.

Learn to shop smart for the Indian cook's time-saving secret ingredients, and discover how to make three great meals with just one storecupboard ingredient.

Feed the family, enjoy Indian tapas with drinks, or create a comforting, easy supper after a busy day at work... it's all here. Anjum's recipes make cooking wonderful Indian food at home both simple and fun.

Quadrille Publishing Ltd
Alhambra House
27–31 Charing Cross Road
London WC2H OLS
www.quadrille.co.uk

QUICK
& EASY
INDIAN

QUICK & EASY INDIAN

ANJUM ANAND

Quadrille
PUBLISHING

This book is dedicated to everyone who cooks home-made meals
in these crazy-busy, convenience-oriented times.

Editorial director Anne Furniss
Creative director Helen Lewis
Editor Lucy Bannell
Designer Lucy Gowans
Photographer Lisa Linder
Props styling Tabitha Hawkins
and Wei Tang
Home economist Joss Herd
Production director
Vincent Smith
Production controller
Leonie Kellman

First published in 2014 by
Quadrille Publishing Limited
Alhambra House
27–31 Charing Cross Road
London WC2H 0LS
www.quadrille.co.uk

Text © 2014 Anjum Anand
Photography © 2014 Lisa Linder
Design and layout © 2014
Quadrille Publishing Limited

Cataloguing in Publication Data:
a catalogue record for this book
is available from the British
Library.

ISBN 978 1 84949 378 9

Printed in China

CONTENTS

INTRODUCTION

Everyone I know is busy. This generation fills each moment of every day. Even our weekends are stuffed with plans. My life has recently become a little busier, with a second child and a new business, and I understand the pressures of juggling life as much as the next person. Something has got to give and, in many people's cases, it is often the cooking. That is a real shame. For me, eating fresh food is still the best way to ensure good health. I do believe you are what you eat and that good, fresh food is imperative for proper well-being. It is good to know what you are putting into your body. Cooking at home is also the most cost-effective option. But meals don't have to be elaborate or time-consuming.

Indian food in my home is continually evolving so, while at its core it remains the food I grew up on, the edges are definitely morphing with my life. The meals I cook are often simple, with lots of one-pot recipes, easy street foods, spice-laced sandwiches, salads and quick curries. This book is a reflection of those meals. There is no compromise on flavour – I always need to enjoy my food – but the recipes are truly where quick and easy meets delicious... and I am really excited for you to try them for yourself.

Take the super-easy Lazy Roast Poussins with Sunshine Saffron Yogurt. This recipe's active time is just five to 10 minutes and you have a great summery meal at the end of it. For both omnivores and herbivores, there are amazing vegetarian meals here: try the light and crispy Butternut, Mushroom and Crème Fraîche Filo Tart. I love desserts and here have given classic Indian puddings made easy, such as Cheat's Rasmalai; fusion creations such as Near-instant Berry, Violet and Star Anise Eton Mess; and the much-coveted – indeed until now secret – My Quick-to-make Almond Cake. There is plenty for everyone.

This book is the perfect way to help you spend less time in the kitchen... if you know what I mean! There are lots of effort- and time-saving tips and ingredients that will cut hours from your cooking time each week. Have a read through and note the recipes that interest you, so you can turn to them in times of mild panic. Remember that the best way to save time is to have the ingredients close to hand, so a little forward planning about what to cook really helps avoid any last-minute scrambles.

I think a lot more people will find time to cook once they are inspired to do so. I truly believe this book provides that inspiration, so you will bounce into the kitchen to produce these meals in no time... then bounce out again and get on with your busy life!

TIME-SAVING INDIAN INGREDIENTS

There are so many products you can buy that will help you cut down on time spent in the kitchen... the only question, really, is how much do you want done for you? I still like to do as much as I can, but there are some time-saving ingredients that I do use all the time, and still others that I think are worth considering.

Crispy fried shallots or onions
I once bought a jar of these from an Oriental supermarket and found them so useful that I now always have them in the cupboard. Leave them whole to enhance biryanis or to add an extra texture to a salad or soup, or crush them and add to curries instead of using fresh onions. I haven't done that in this book, but it is an easy way to add sweetness, particularly if you use the onions rather than the shallots. Buying these will of course save you 10 minutes or so of slicing and frying... but really they are much more useful than that.

Tamarind and date chutney
This thick, dark, sweet treasure is one of India's most popular chutneys. Similar to ketchup in its versatility, Indians use it in just the same way as a condiment and dip, but it is also mixed into snacks and street foods. I used to make my own, but these days I also buy it in. I haven't tried every type on the market, but I do like the Maggi brand, sold as tamarind 'sauce'. A fantastic time- and effort-saver!

Ready-cooked rice
Although rice only takes eight minutes once the water is boiling, it does add another element to cook in your meal. There are now very good ready-cooked rices that only require reheating and they can be used in any of the rice dishes in this book. They are often sold in 250g packs, which equates to about 95g of raw rice, so you can estimate the amount you will need (though be aware that it will depend on the type and age of the rice, so it is impossible to be exact). Omit the rice-cooking process from any of my rice recipes and stir the ready-cooked rice into the flavoured oil or base (which needs to be fully cooked).

Pani puri packets and kits

Pani puri is a most delicious Indian street food snack of crispy thin-skinned spheres of pastry filled with any combination of ingredients, topped with a sweet, sour and spicy liquid and popped straight into your mouth. They are really, truly delicious. You can now find packets of the puri (the spheres) as well as the pani (the spices and sauces that go into the liquid), or you can buy whole kits with everything you need inside. Pani puri are excellent quick bites to whet the appetite and the kits are definitely worth buying (see page 12 for my favourite version).

Rice paper wrappers

These are so versatile that I have been using them for a long time now. The longer I have them, the more uses I find for them, so in this book I have included some delicious and easy recipes. They only need a five- to 10-second soak before they can be eaten, so are minimal effort. Buy them in Oriental supermarkets and online.

Frozen grated coconut and creamed coconut

I always have a packet of frozen grated coconut that I buy from my Indian shop. It is kept in the freezer and bits are chiselled off as needed. It is by far the easiest way to get fresh coconut into your meals. You can buy it online as well. A block of creamed coconut is not a new revolutionary ingredient, but it has recently had a resurgence in my kitchen. I hate wasting 400g cans of coconut milk that only get partially used, and refuse to add the whole thing just because I have it. So creamed coconut really works for me. Store it in the fridge and grate or chop off as much as you need for a recipe. It is not as sweet as coconut milk and I find it has more texture. It is easy to find in supermarkets and well-stocked local shops.

Ginger and garlic pastes

I have to confess, I do not use these as I always have ginger and garlic at home and it takes just minutes to grate, but I know a lot of very good Indian cooks who do, so feel free to use them if you find them more convenient.

Paneer

This Indian white cheese can be bought in supermarkets as well as online. Soak in just-boiled water for 10 minutes to soften it before using. If you want to make your own, which will be more tender (though obviously not time-saving!), see page 50.

Useful online stockists

itadka.com for most Indian groceries, fresh and dried (London area only)
spicesofindia.co.uk for most Indian ingredients
theasiancookshop.co.uk for most Asian ingredients

INDIAN TAPAS

Avocado pani puri

Pani puri is a fabulous street-food snack. A hollow, crispy shell is half-filled with, traditionally, chickpeas or sprouted pulses and chopped potato, a tangy, minty and slightly sweet liquid is poured in, then the whole thing is popped straight into the mouth where it bursts into a firework of flavours and textures. There are lots of pani puri kits in Indian grocery shops these days. If you buy one of those, follow the instructions on the packet to make the liquid. I buy the individual elements, so this recipe is based on that.

You can vary the fillings, or keep it traditional. I have used an avocado 'salsa' for a creamy but crunchy twist and, for the non-vegetarian variety, I've added salmon roe and a touch of sour cream for added luxury. Both are super-easy to make and stonkingly good.

First make the tamarind and mint liquid. Pour 250ml of water into a bowl and stir in the pani puri masala powder, tamarind sauce or chutney and the mint. Adjust the balance of flavourings to taste, adding more tamarind chutney for sweet sourness, or masala powder for spiciness.

Mix together the avocado and the lime zest and juice, tossing gently but thoroughly to coat the avocado and stop it from discolouring. Add all the other ingredients for the filling. Taste and adjust the salt.

When you are ready to eat, crack a hole with your finger into the thinner surface of a pani puri shell (one side will always be thinner and more delicate). Add about 1 tsp of the filling to the cavity and place on a serving platter. Repeat to use up all the shells and filling.

When you are ready to eat, pour the tamarind liquid into a small jug and place next to your puris. Before eating one, pour 3–4 tsp of the liquid into the hole and place in your mouth (it will leak everywhere otherwise). Enjoy!

and a salmon roe version...
Top the filling of each pani puri with about
1 tsp salmon roe and add a little sour cream

Makes 20

for the spiced tamarind and mint liquid
1 tbsp store-bought pani puri
   masala powder, or to taste
4 tbsp store-bought tamarind
   sauce (I like Maggi brand),
   or home-made Quick Tamarind
   Chutney (see page 155),
   or to taste
8 mint leaves, finely shredded

for the filling
1 ripe avocado, finely chopped
finely grated zest of ½ lime,
   plus 2 tsp lime juice
1 small tomato, finely chopped
1 spring onion, finely chopped
½ small red onion,
   finely chopped
½–1 small red chilli, deseeded
   and finely chopped
small handful of chopped
   coriander leaves
salt

20 pani puri shells

time-saving star: *pani puri shells*

Speedy spiced tomato bruschetta with herbed yogurt

These are seriously delicious; only once I took my first bite did I really appreciate how all the flavours and textures would come together. By writing this, I realise I am setting your expectations really high, so I hope you love them as much as I do! They are a lovely, easy starter, but also great for brunch with a poached egg on top (with or without the yogurt).

Brush both sides of the slices of sourdough with the oil, then griddle on a hot griddle pan until golden. Rub one side of each slice with the garlic clove and set the toasts aside in a warm place.

Mix the coriander and chilli into the yogurt and season to taste.

Heat the 1 tbsp of oil in a very small pan and add the panch phoran. Once the spluttering starts to subside, add the tomatoes, sugar and salt to taste. Cook until the tomatoes are heated through and softening, two to four minutes.

Assemble the bruschetta: divide the tomato mixture into six equal portions. Pile each portion on to a slice of the bread and top with 1 tbsp of the yogurt mixture. Serve immediately.

Makes 6

6 thin slices of sourdough bread
1 tbsp olive oil, plus more for
  the bread
1 fat garlic clove, halved
small handful of chopped
  coriander leaves
1 small green chilli,
  finely chopped
120g Greek yogurt
salt and freshly ground
  black pepper
1 rounded tsp panch phoran
  (or see page 122 for how to
  make your own)
3 tomatoes, sliced into
  thin wedges
good pinch of caster sugar

10 mins to cook

Tangy mushroom fritters

In the carnivorous world of kebab eaters, vegetarians usually get a raw deal. But North Indians make kebabs of everything; not merely skewered meat but any 'meaty' bite-sized snack. These mushroom fritters are based on spicy meat kebabs, but do not feel at all like a poor impersonation. They stand proud and are full of flavour. As with other kebabs, you can serve these with Tangy Coriander Chutney (see page 154), but a simple topping of roast red pepper and a dab of sour cream is an easy, effective alternative. The mushroom mix can be made in advance and cooked when you are ready to eat.

Heat a large, non-stick sauté pan with 1 tbsp of the oil and add the mushrooms with some salt. Stir-fry until the liquid released by the mushrooms has evaporated and they have started to colour. Add the ginger and garlic and cook for another minute or until the garlic is cooked through. Take off the heat and allow to cool for five minutes or so.

Place a small, dry frying pan over a medium heat and spoon in the gram flour. Cook, stirring constantly, until it turns a shade darker and smells slightly toasty. Tip it into the mushrooms and add the spices, yogurt, chilli (if using), coriander, spring onion and 4 tbsp of the breadcrumbs. Stir, then taste and adjust the seasoning. Tip the remaining breadcrumbs into a broad shallow dish or large plate.

When ready to eat, make 5cm burger-like patties of the mushroom mixture and dip both sides into the remaining breadcrumbs. Heat half the remaining oil in a large, non-stick sauté pan over a medium heat and add half the fritters to the pan, being careful not to crowd it. Fry over a medium heat until golden, then flip over and fry the other side until it, too, is golden. Place on kitchen paper to absorb any excess oil while you fry the remaining fritters in the remaining oil. Serve hot.

Makes 15 small fritters

4 tbsp vegetable oil
400g mushrooms, finely chopped (I use 50–60 per cent shiitake with the rest chestnut or oyster)
salt and lots of freshly ground black pepper
15g root ginger, peeled weight, finely chopped
6 fat garlic cloves, finely chopped
50g gram (chickpea) flour
3 tsp mango powder (*amchoor*)
2 tsp garam masala
2 tsp roasted ground cumin (see page 92)
2 tbsp Greek yogurt
a little chopped green chilli (optional)
small fistful of chopped coriander leaves
1 spring onion, finely sliced
4 slices of bread, made into crumbs

Five-minute garlic, chilli and coriander prawns

Prawns make everything taste good, as do garlic, chilli and butter, so this dish is clearly going to be a winner all round. Serve with crusty bread on the side. The flavoured butter can be made in advance and kept in the fridge.

Mash the garlic, chilli and coriander into the butter.

Heat a sauté pan. Add the butter and heat until it melts, then throw in the nigella seeds, prawns and a little seasoning and stir-fry until the prawns are pink all over and cooked through, a matter of two or three minutes. Squeeze over some lemon juice and serve with lemon wedges on the side.

Serves 6–8 as part of a mixed tapas

5 fat garlic cloves, grated
½–¾ red chilli, finely chopped
large handful of finely chopped
  coriander leaves and stalks
100g unsalted butter, softened
½ tsp nigella seeds
600g raw tiger prawns, shelled
  but tail left on, deveined
salt and freshly ground
  black pepper
1 lemon, plus lemon wedges
  to serve

10 mins to cook

PACK OF RICE PAPER WRAPPERS

Just a quick soak in a dish of water and these
beautifully translucent, crisp rice paper circles become
supple and delicious. Like me, you will soon
find you are wrapping everything up in them.
And they last for ages in the cupboard.

Duck kathi rolls

'Kathi kebab', 'Nizam rolls' and 'frankies' are all names for the same species of Indian street
food snack: a wrap with a spiced, tangy filling, often containing still-crunchy onions and
softened tomatoes. This is my light, simple version and it makes a perfect, pretty bite-sized
Indian tapa. You can substitute the duck for lamb or chicken, if you prefer. You can buy rice
paper wrappers in large packets and, as I have found so many uses for them, I think that it is
absolutely worth buying them in bulk and having them to hand. Serve these as they are, or
with a small bowl of Tangy Coriander Chutney (see page 154).

Heat 1½ tbsp of the oil in a large non-stick frying pan. Add the ginger and garlic,
reduce the heat and stir-fry for about a minute until the garlic is starting to colour.
Add the onion, duck, spices and only a little salt (because the chaat masala is
salty). Stir-fry for one minute, then add the tomato and fry for another minute.
Taste and adjust the seasoning and spices to taste. Take off the heat.

Fill a large bowl or plate with water. Soak the rice paper wrappers individually for
about 30 seconds or until soft and pliable. Once soft, place a wrapper in front of
you on kitchen paper. Place four or five carrot batons in the centre with one of the
chopped sprigs of coriander. Top with slivers of duck, making sure you include the
onions, tomatoes and their spicy juices. Make a parcel by folding over the edge
of the wrapper closest to you, then fold in both sides, then finally roll away from
you into a parcel. Place on a plate, seam underneath, with the colourful vegetables
clearly seen through the wrapper on top. Make the rest in the same way.

When they are all done, heat the remaining oil in a large frying pan until quite hot.
Place the rolls in, seam-side down, and cook for one or two minutes or until the
bottom is crisp. Serve.

Makes 8

2 tbsp vegetable oil
15g root ginger, peeled
  weight, grated
3 fat garlic cloves, grated
1 small red onion, finely sliced
175g skinless duck breasts,
  sliced on the diagonal into
  5cm-long slices
1 rounded tsp ground cumin,
  or to taste
1 rounded tsp chaat masala,
  or to taste
½ tsp freshly ground black
  pepper, or to taste
salt
1 small vine tomato, sliced
8 rice paper wrappers
1 large carrot, peeled and cut
  into thin batons
8 sprigs of coriander, washed
  and cut into 5cm lengths

Quick masala 'dosas'

Dosas are crisp, spongy pancakes made with a fermented lentil and rice batter. They are lovely, but far from quick and easy to make! So, at home, I've started using these rice paper wrappers instead of the pancakes. They make light and crispy envelopes but, unlike true dosas, are not the main event, rather just the wrapping for this lovely, spiced potato filling. These make a substantial, satisfying main course as well as a tapa if the portion size is increased. Either way, I serve them with Coastal Coconut Chutney (see page 154); it whizzes up quickly if you have some frozen grated coconut stashed away, which I highly recommend.

Peel the potatoes and cut into 5cm cubes. Place in a pan of water and boil until just cooked.

After about 10 minutes, heat the 3–4 tbsp of oil in a large non-stick frying pan. Add the mustard seeds and, once the popping starts to die down, add the chillies and chana dal and, after about 10 seconds, follow with the urad dal. Cook until the lentils start to colour, then add the curry leaves, onions and salt. Cook the onions over a medium-low flame until just caramelising on the edges.

Meanwhile, check the potatoes. When done, remove with a slotted spoon (reserve the liquid in the pan). Once the onions are done, add 1–2 tbsp of water from the potato pan and the turmeric and cook for 20 seconds.

Add the potatoes, seasoning and lemon juice to the frying pan and press down with a masher to coarsely mash the potatoes; there should be large pieces as well as some mashed bits. Add more of the potato cooking water if the mixture seems a bit dry, it should come together in clumps. Taste, adjust the seasoning and add the peanuts. Take off the heat and pour away the remaining potato cooking water.

When ready to assemble, fill a large bowl or plate with water. Soak the rice paper wrappers individually for about 30 seconds, or until soft and pliable. Once soft, place a wrapper in front of you on kitchen paper. Place about 3 tbsp of the potato filling across the centre in a thick log. Make a parcel by folding over the edge of the wrapper closest to you, then fold in both sides, then finally roll away from you to make a thick sausage shape. Repeat with the remaining wrappers and filling. You can serve them now, or you can fry them if you like, as follows.

If you want to fry the rolls, wipe the pan you were cooking in and add 2 tsp of the remaining oil. Add five of the rolls, seam-side up, and cook gently until golden, then flip over and cook the seam side until golden. Repeat with the rest of the oil and rolls, then serve.

Makes 10

500g (2 medium) potatoes
3–4 tbsp vegetable oil, plus
  4 tsp to cook the
  rolls (optional)
1½ tsp mustard seeds
2–4 dried red chillies (optional)
2 rounded tsp *chana dal*
  (Bengal gram)
2 rounded tsp *urad dal*
  (skinned black gram)
12 fresh curry leaves
2 onions, sliced
salt and freshly ground
  black pepper
½ tsp turmeric
4 tsp lemon juice
5 tbsp roasted salted peanuts
10 rice paper wrappers

TAKE

Southern-spiced Vietnamese crab spring rolls

I love these: they are light, full of flavour and really easy. You can make up the filling ahead and roll it in the rice paper wrappers close to the time of serving, then keep them covered with a damp tea towel on a plate in the fridge.

Makes 8

200g mixed brown and white crab meat
15g root ginger, peeled weight, finely chopped
3 tsp finely chopped red chillies (2–3 chillies)
salt and a good pinch of freshly ground black pepper
finely grated zest of 1 small unwaxed lemon, plus
4 tbsp lemon juice
40g grated coconut (I buy frozen grated coconut and allow it to defrost)
8 rice paper wrappers
7.5cm length of cucumber, deseeded and cut into julienne
7.5cm length of carrot, peeled and cut into julienne

Place the crab in a large bowl. Heat the oil in a small saucepan and add the mustard seeds. As they sizzle, add the curry leaves. Reduce the heat and add the ginger and chillies, cook for 10 seconds, then turn the heat off. Pour the contents of the saucepan into the crab with the black pepper, lemon zest and juice and coconut. Stir well and season to taste with salt.

When ready to serve, fill a large bowl or plate with water. Soak the rice paper wrappers individually for about 30 seconds or until soft and pliable. Once soft, place a wrapper in front of you on kitchen paper. Put about one-eighth of each of the cucumber and carrot across the centre of the wrapper in a line and top with one-eighth of the crab mixture. Make a parcel by folding over the edge of the wrapper closest to you, then fold in both sides, then finally roll away from you into a firm cigar shape. Repeat with the remaining filling and rice paper wrappers. Cut each roll in half on the diagonal and serve.

time-saving star: frozen grated coconut

Spiced seafood samosas

These are lovely small treats to have with drinks, but also elegant enough to serve as a starter with a little salad and chutney on the side. I like to use a mixture of prawns, squid, mussels, salmon and white fish (you can buy mixes at a fishmonger or supermarket fish counter), but use fewer varieties if that is easier for you. I sometimes add desiccated coconut to the filling as well. If you don't have dried mango powder, use lemon juice, and add a few extra breadcrumbs to the filling to soak up its moisture.

Makes 20 small cocktail-sized samosas

4 tbsp vegetable oil, plus more to deep-fry
1 onion, very finely chopped
15g root ginger, peeled weight, grated
4 large garlic cloves, grated
4 tsp tomato purée
500g mixed raw seafood and fish, coarsely chopped (see recipe introduction)
⅔ tsp freshly ground black pepper
salt
1 tsp garam masala
4 tbsp breadcrumbs
1 large red chilli, finely chopped
2 tsp mango powder (*amchoor*), or to taste
20 x 7.5cm-wide store-bought samosa strips
5 tbsp plain flour

Heat the oil in a large non-stick sauté pan. Add the onion and cook until turning golden on the edges. Tip in the ginger and garlic and sauté gently for a minute or two. Add the tomato purée and cook out for a minute, then add the seafood, seasoning and garam masala and sauté for three minutes. Stir in the breadcrumbs, chilli and mango powder, then taste and adjust the seasoning.

To assemble the samosas, peel off a samosa strip and place it with the short end facing you. Place 1 tbsp of the filling on the bottom of the strip closest to you, leaving a 1cm border. Now fold over the right-hand corner of the strip so that it encloses the filling to make a triangle (see image). Then keep folding the filled triangle upwards until you have a small piece of spare wrapper left at the end. Mix the flour in a cup with enough water to make a thickish, gluey paste. Using a pastry brush or your fingers, spread this flour paste over the spare piece of samosa wrapper and fold over to seal the samosa. Brush any loose edges with the floury paste, again to enclose. Repeat with the remaining filling and wrappers.

Heat enough oil to be about 7.5cm deep in a wok, karahi (the Indian version of a wok) or saucepan until it either reaches 180°C/350°F on an oil thermometer, or a piece of bread starts to bubble as soon as you put it in. Add four or five samosas, but do not overcrowd the pan, and fry, turning once, until golden on both sides, around two minutes in total. Remove and drain on kitchen paper. Repeat with the remaining samosas and serve hot.

time-saving star: samosa strips

Malai chicken tikka

Malai is the cream that rises to the surface of a bottle of milk. Indian housewives would collect this, skimming it off until they had enough to do something special with it, such as this creamy grilled chicken. It is succulent with a delicate flavour that tastes like special occasion food, but so easy to make that it is almost an everyday meal. It's lovely as a tapa with other dishes or as a starter. Serve with Tangy Coriander Chutney (see page 154), or just with a salad. You can marinate it ahead of time and simply cook it when you are ready to eat.

Mix the garlic, ginger, salt and pepper into the chicken in a shallow dish, cover and allow to marinate for at least 30 minutes.

Mix the remaining marinade ingredients together and add to the chicken. Mix well, cover, place in the fridge and allow to marinate for at least one hour. Meanwhile, soak the bamboo skewers in water for at least 30 minutes; this will stop them scorching when you come to cook the chicken.

When ready to cook, preheat the oven to 220°C/425°F/gas mark 7 and return the chicken to room temperature. Drain the skewers and thread the chicken on to them, dividing it equally.

Place the skewers on a baking tray lined with foil and roast for six to eight minutes. They will brown in places and release lots of liquid. Baste with this liquid as much as possible. Check if they are cooked through by piercing a large piece of chicken to its centre: if the juices run clear, they are ready. If there is any trace of pink, cook for another minute or two, then check again. Serve immediately, with a salad on the side.

Serves 4 as a starter or 8 as part of a mixed tapas

for the marinade
3 fat garlic cloves, grated
20g root ginger, peeled
   weight, grated
¾ tsp salt
½ tsp freshly ground
   black pepper
⅓ tsp ground cardamom
⅓ tsp ground mace
⅓ tsp grated nutmeg
100ml double cream
40g finely grated
   Cheddar cheese
2 tsp cornflour
3 tbsp Greek yogurt

for the chicken skewers
4 skinless boneless chicken
   thighs, cut into large chunks
8 bamboo skewers

Nepalese chicken momos with tomato, chilli and ginger dipping sauce

These are delicious, healthy and fun to make... and you can cheat by using store-bought wonton wrappers instead of making your own. Momos are Chinese-inspired dumplings that made their way to India from Nepal. I have been obsessed by momos ever since I watched a Nepalese lady knock up a great, tasty dinner for herself in 15 minutes. I learned how to make them years later and have never looked back. You don't have to have years of dumpling-making experience, so give them a try; I guarantee you will love them. You can also serve them with a little chilli-flecked soy sauce instead of the more traditional dipping sauce below.

Put a steamer on to boil filled with 5cm of water. Oil the steamer basket well.

If you want to make the dough, mix the flour and 5–6 tbsp of water. Give it a good knead so that it is smooth and soft. Place it under a damp tea towel and allow to rest while you make the filling. Or just use a packet of wonton wrappers.

Mix together all the ingredients for the filling, seasoning with salt as you do. Fry off a tiny bit, taste it to check for seasoning and adjust as necessary.

If you made the dough, pinch off a large marble-sized piece. Cover the rest with the tea towel again as you work. Using only a tiny bit of flour – and only when it is necessary – roll out each ball into a very thin circle. It should be 6.5–7.5cm in diameter. Or place a wonton wrapper in front of you. Place a generous teaspoonful of filling in the centre and enclose it: I take the momo in my right hand and use my thumb and forefinger to gather the edges of the dough and pleat as I stick them together. Keep the filling away from the seam. Place the momos on the oiled steamer basket, seam-side up. Repeat with the remaining filling and wrappers.

Once they are all done, steam for 12 minutes, or until the dough is no longer sticky. Serve hot with Tomato, Chilli and Ginger Dipping Sauce (see below).

Quick-fire: Tomato, chilli and ginger dipping sauce
Heat a griddle pan and add 2 large quartered tomatoes and 1 large red chilli (or to taste). Cook, turning, until the skins blacken. Heat 1 tsp of vegetable oil in a small saucepan and fry 2 finely chopped garlic cloves for one minute until just cooked, removing from the heat before they colour. Pour into a blender, or a jug. Skin the tomatoes and chilli as far as possible and add them to the blender or jug. Blend, or whizz with a hand-held blender, adding 1–2 tbsp of water, to a smooth sauce. Add a pinch of caster sugar, 10g finely chopped root ginger and ⅓ tsp red wine vinegar and season with salt to taste. Makes enough to serve with the momos.

Makes 20–22

for the filling
1 tbsp vegetable oil, plus more for the steamer basket
200g minced chicken, or 2 skinless boneless thighs or 1 large breast, finely chopped
½ onion, finely chopped
2 fat garlic cloves, grated
12g root ginger, peeled weight, grated
60g carrot, finely grated, moisture squeezed out
4 tbsp chopped coriander leaves
½ tsp freshly ground black pepper
¾ tsp garam masala
¾ tsp ground cumin
salt

for the dough (optional)
100g plain flour, plus more to dust, or just use store-bought wonton wrappers

time-saving star: wonton wrappers

Griddled Bihari beef skewers

This dish is based on a well-loved Indian kebab, with spicing that is mild enough to reveal and not overpower the flavour of the meat. I have used feather blade of beef which comes from the shoulder, is inexpensive, tender and really quick to cook.

You can serve these with Tangy Coriander Chutney (see page 154), or a sweeter mint chutney, or simply just as they are with some salad. For extra succulent, tender meat, try marinating the beef in 4 tbsp green papaya paste (see page 84).

There is usually cartilage running horizontally through the centre of the steak, so, to prepare the meat, thinly slice it (around ½cm thick) across the grain, then slice off pieces on either side of the cartilage so that you have cartilage-free strips of meat. Discard the cartilage. If your piece of beef doesn't conform to this standard, simply cut it into cubes, avoiding any hard bits.

Pour the vegetable oil into a small frying pan over a medium heat and fry the onion until golden brown. Add the garlic and cook for another minute or until soft. Scrape these into a blender with the ground spices, seasoning, ginger and yogurt and blend until smooth, or use a hand-held blender. Taste and adjust the seasoning. Coat the strips of meat with this marinade in a shallow dish, cover and leave for at least one hour (or overnight; the longer the better) in the fridge.

Return the meat to room temperature before cooking. Meanwhile, soak the bamboo skewers in water for at least 30 minutes. This will stop them scorching when you cook the meat.

Heat up a large griddle pan. Divide the pieces of meat between the drained skewers and place on the griddle pan. Cook, without disturbing, for one or two minutes, then turn and repeat on the next side. There should be some lovely charred griddle marks on your meat.

Serve immediately with lemon wedges, Tangy Coriander Chutney (see page 154), or a mint chutney, and a salad on the side for crunch.

Makes 8 skewers

400g feather blade of beef
1 tbsp vegetable oil
1 small onion, sliced
4 fat garlic cloves, sliced
1 rounded tsp garam masala
¾ tsp roasted ground cumin
  (see page 92)
¼ tsp chilli powder, or to taste
⅔ tsp salt and lots of freshly
  ground black pepper
20g root ginger, peeled weight,
  coarsely chopped
4 tbsp plain yogurt
8 bamboo skewers
lemon wedges, to serve

FAST
FAMILY FOOD

Grilled cheese and Indian chutney

India has never had a sandwich culture to rival that of the West but, wherever you travel in the country, you will probably notice a chutney sandwich for sale. At its purest it is simply tangy green chutney, cucumber and tomato slices on white bread, untoasted. I find these sandwiches so addictive that I have been making them at home for years. This is my embellished version. I like mine with a little mayo for an unctuous creaminess, but my husband prefers his with butter. Use whichever you prefer.

Butter – or spread a little mayonnaise on – one slice of bread. Add the lettuce, tomato, red onion (if using) and cheese. Sprinkle with the capers (if using). Spread the chutney on the other slice of bread and place on top of the cheese.

Toast the sandwich in a press, if you have one. Otherwise, place a small frying pan over a medium heat and oil it very lightly. Grill the sandwich in the hot pan, pressing down with a fish slice or a broad spatula until golden brown and crisp, then turn and repeat on the other side. It will be warm and melting in the middle.

Makes 1

softened butter or light mayonnaise, to taste

2 slices of bread (whatever you have or like)

1–2 leaves crispy green lettuce

½ small ripe tomato, finely sliced

1 tbsp finely chopped red onion (optional)

1 large, thin slice of cheese (at least large enough to cover your slice of bread)

1 tsp capers, drained and rinsed well (optional)

3 tbsp Tangy Coriander Chutney (see page 154)

a little vegetable oil (optional)

Smoked mackerel-in-a-minute tartines

This is a dead fast, light meal that delivers well above its effort quotient on flavour and texture. I like to use dark rye bread as it works with the smokiness of the fish and the creaminess of the crème fraîche, but use whichever bread you like, as long as it is robust so that it will retain its structure. The pomegranate seeds add a lovely fresh astringency that complements the fish, but you can leave them out if you prefer.

Start with the pickled cucumber. Mix together all the ingredients except the cucumber, until the sugar has dissolved, then mix in the cucumber. Leave for 15 minutes, for the flavours to come together and the cucumber to pickle lightly.

Now for the tartines. Mix the coriander, spring onion and chilli into the crème fraîche along with a little seasoning. Dollop half of this mixture on each slice of bread, spreading it thickly and evenly.

Remove the skin and roughly flake the flesh of the fish into large chunks and place evenly on the crème fraîche. Drain the cucumber and scatter it over the fish. Do the same with the pomegranate seeds, then serve.

Makes 2, can be doubled

For the pickled cucumber
2 tbsp white wine vinegar
$\frac{1}{2}$ tsp caster sugar
$\frac{1}{4}$ tsp coriander seeds, lightly crushed
pinch of salt
5cm cucumber, halved lengthways, deseeded and sliced into julienne

For the tartines
small handful of chopped coriander leaves
1 small spring onion, finely chopped
$\frac{1}{4}$–$\frac{1}{2}$ small Indian green 'finger' chilli, finely chopped
4 tbsp crème fraîche (can be light)
freshly ground black pepper
2 slices of rye bread (pumpernickel) or other
2 smoked mackerel fillets
handful of pomegranate seeds

Warm chicken tikka sandwich

I first came across a tandoori chicken sandwich 20 years ago in a hotel in India and it opened my mind to the humble sandwich, then largely a vehicle used to empty the fridge of cold bits. It was made with love... and it showed. This recipe is based on those memories. You can cheat and buy a tikka paste (or even a whole tandoori chicken). But scale the recipe up to cook a whole bird at home and this chicken will solve a multitude of lunch and lunch box quandaries.

Pierce the chicken with a fork all over, whether using thighs or breasts. If you are using chicken breasts, slash the thicker parts at 2cm intervals. If you have time, marinate the chicken now in a shallow dish with half each of the salt, lemon juice, ginger and garlic for the tandoori paste, for 20 minutes. This will help to tenderise the meat.

Blend together all the ingredients for the tandoori paste until smooth (with or without the first marinade ingredients, depending on whether you have used them), not forgetting the salt. Place the chicken in a dish (or keep it in the same one, if you have already marinated it). Pour over the marinade, turn the chicken to coat, cover, place in the fridge and marinate it for as long as you can; at least for one hour and up to overnight. Return to room temperature before cooking.

When ready to cook, preheat the oven to 200°C/400°F/gas mark 6. Place a baking tray or some foil under an oven rack. Place the chicken straight on the rack and bake for 15 minutes or until done; when you pierce the thickest part of a chicken piece, the juices that emerge should run clear with no trace of pink. If it's not quite ready, cook for a few minutes longer, then test again. Take the chicken out of the oven and leave to rest on the baking tray or foil that collected the juices.

Place the baguette or slices of bread in the oven to warm up a little for a few minutes. Cut or tear the chicken into large pieces.

Butter one side of the baguette or two slices of the bread and layer on the tomato, lettuce and red onion. Slather the chutney over the other side or slices of bread. Place the chicken on the vegetables, close your sandwich and eat it while it's hot!

Makes 2

For the sandwich
2 skinless boneless chicken thighs or small breasts
small baguette, or 4 slices of sourdough bread
soft butter
1 plum tomato, sliced
2–3 crisp lettuce leaves
¼ small red onion, finely sliced
4–6 tbsp Tangy Coriander Chutney (see page 154)

For the tandoori paste
⅓ tsp salt
1 tbsp lemon juice
5g root ginger, peeled weight, grated
1 fat garlic clove, grated
65g Greek yogurt
½ tsp chilli powder
1 tsp paprika (optional, as it's just for colour)
¾ tsp ground cumin
1 tbsp vegetable oil
½ tsp garam masala
1 rounded tsp tomato purée

Rare is the fridge that does not contain a yogurt pot. It's a safe bet, ready to become an instant pudding – with fruit added – or a topping for granola. But yogurt has a far more glamorous potential. It can make bread dreamily light, and in a marinade will add tanginess and break down fibres to give super-tender meat. So come on, make your yogurt pot work harder for your family.

Tandoori roast salmon tacos

This is such a delicious, light but satisfying meal, you will want to eat it day after day. The flavours are at once herby, spicy, tangy and creamy with every mouthful having a little smooth and a little crunch. You can use Indian breads instead of tortillas, or go naked and leave the bread/tortillas out entirely.

Mix all the ingredients for the marinade, adding 5 tbsp of the yogurt for the tacos, and season well. It should taste tangy, spicy and salty, as the fish will absorb it and each piece will only have a light coating. Add the fish, turn to coat and, if you have time, cover and leave to marinate for 30 minutes in the fridge. Don't leave it much longer, or the yogurt can affect the texture of the salmon.

Meanwhile, make the slaw. Heat the oil in a large, non-stick frying pan. Add the seeds and, once they have popped, add the vegetables and seasoning. Cook over a high heat for three to four minutes, stirring once or twice, then take off the heat.

When ready to cook, preheat the oven to 220°C/425°F/gas mark 7.

Place the fish on an oiled baking tray and cook for eight minutes, or until it starts to separate into flakes when prodded and has charred on the surface. At the same time, wrap the tortillas (if using) in foil and place on the bottom of the oven as your fish cooks.

Bring all the ingredients separately to the table for everyone to help themselves. To assemble this in a tortilla, I spread a generous amount of the chutney over the tortilla, top with the avocado, the slaw and then the fish, with a big dollop of yogurt next to it. Fold and eat.

Serves 4

For the marinade
2 garlic cloves, grated
20g root ginger, peeled weight, grated
3 tbsp lemon juice
1½ tsp ground cumin
2 tbsp gram (chickpea) flour
1¼ tsp chilli powder
¾ tsp carom seeds
2 tsp dried fenugreek leaves, crushed in your fingers
1 tbsp vegetable oil, plus more for the tray
salt and freshly ground black pepper

For the fish tacos
175g Greek yogurt
4 thick salmon fillets
8 small corn or 4 large flour tortillas (optional, see recipe introduction)
8 tbsp Tangy Coriander Chutney (see page 154)
1 small avocado, finely sliced

For the warm cabbage slaw
1 tbsp vegetable oil
⅔ tsp brown mustard seeds
⅔ tsp nigella seeds
160g red cabbage, shredded
80g carrots, finely sliced into long shreds
1 small red onion, finely sliced

Spiced pepper and feta cornbread

In rural Punjab, they have an amazing meal which consists of a combination of local greens cooked into a mash with lots of butter, accompanied by fried maize flatbreads. This got me thinking about a modern, easier version of the flatbread... which took me to one of my favourite things: cornbread. I have spiced it up and it's absolutely wonderful. This works so well with so many different dishes in the book. Try it with Smoky Hot Lentils (see overleaf).

Preheat the oven to 200°C/400°F/gas mark 6. Line a 23cm round springform cake tin with baking parchment.

Heat the oil in a small non-stick saucepan. Add the cumin seeds and, once they're aromatic, add the spring onions, pepper, chilli and butter and cook for four or five minutes, or until the pepper is soft.

Mix together the polenta, flour, baking powder, salt and bicarbonate of soda and make a well in the middle. Mix together the eggs, yogurt and milk in a jug and pour into the well, whisking together to amalgamate. Stir in the contents of the red pepper saucepan and the feta and pour into the prepared tin.

Bake for 20–25 minutes, or until a cocktail stick inserted into the centre of the cake comes out with moist crumbs attached to it. Remove from the oven and set aside until cool enough to handle. Take it out of the tin, remove the baking parchment and cut into wedges to serve.

Serves 8–10

1 tbsp vegetable oil
1 tsp cumin seeds
4 small spring onions, chopped
½ large red pepper, chopped
1 green chilli, finely chopped
25g unsalted butter
125g fine polenta
125g plain flour, sifted
2 tsp baking powder
⅔ tsp fine sea salt
½ tsp bicarbonate of soda
2 eggs
100g plain yogurt
200ml whole milk
75g feta cheese, or other
  characterful cheese, crumbled

Flying chicken wings

This is such a fabulous recipe that it is great for midweek meals as well as for casual weekend get-togethers for friends or family. There are two stages to the dish, but it is really easy to make. Lovely with some simple vegetables, potatoes or salad.

Mix together all the spices, seasoning, yogurt and the grated ginger and garlic. Pierce the chicken all over, place it in a shallow dish, pour over the marinade, turn to coat, then cover and marinate for 20 minutes, or up to a couple of hours if you have time.

When you're ready to cook, preheat the oven to 220°C/425°F/gas mark 7. Return the chicken wings to room temperature while you find an ovenproof baking dish big enough to hold them snugly in one layer. Arrange the wings in the dish and cook in the oven for 30 minutes, turning every 10 minutes.

After the first turn, heat up the oil in a small saucepan. Add the chopped ginger and garlic, the chillies and curry leaves and cook gently until the garlic is cooked, about one minute. Stir well into the chicken for its remaining cooking time.

Serve hot, with lemon wedges to squeeze over.

Serves 3, can be doubled

½ tsp turmeric
½ tsp chilli powder
1 rounded tsp ground cumin
1 rounded tsp ground coriander
salt and freshly ground
  black pepper
150g plain yogurt
20g root ginger, peeled
  weight: half grated; half
  finely chopped
7 fat garlic cloves: 2 grated;
  5 finely chopped
8 chicken wings, wing tips cut
  off (keep them for stock)
2 tbsp vegetable oil
4–6 green finger chillies,
  pierced with the tip of a knife
12 fresh curry leaves
lemon wedges, to serve

Smoky hot lentils

This is lovely on its own or as an accompaniment, and particularly good with Spiced Pepper and Feta Cornbread (see page 41). It is a very well-behaved recipe that won't mind being made earlier in the day (it only takes 25 minutes), then reheated when you are ready to eat.

Place the lentils in a saucepan, just cover with water and bring to the boil. Reduce the heat to a simmer and cook until al dente, 20–25 minutes.

Meanwhile, heat the oil in a non-stick saucepan. Add the onions and cook over a medium-high heat for three or four minutes (I use this time to grate the garlic and ginger and chop the tomatoes). Add the garlic and ginger to the pan and cook, stirring often, for one minute, or until the garlic no longer smells raw. If it sticks, add a little splash of water from the kettle. Add the tomatoes, some salt and all the spices and cook for five or six minutes or until the whole thing comes together into a mass. Taste; it should taste harmonious. Add another small splash of water from the kettle if the pan seems too dry.

Once the lentils have cooked, drain them, but reserve their liquor. Add the lentils to the spiced tomato pan with the cabbage (if using) and a little of the lentil cooking water: it should be a loose dish, but not a curry. Stir for two or three minutes until the cabbage wilts, then taste, adjust the seasoning and paprika and serve.

Serves 4–5

300g Puy lentils
3–4 tbsp vegetable oil
2 smallish onions, chopped
4 fat garlic cloves, grated
10g root ginger, peeled
  weight, grated
3 tomatoes, blended until
  smooth, or chopped
salt
2 tsp ground coriander
2 tsp ground cumin
1 tsp smoked paprika, or to
  taste (I like a little more,
  but it is strong)
1 tsp garam masala
$\frac{1}{3}$ tsp chilli powder, or
  to taste
2 handfuls of shredded green
  cabbage (optional)

Lazy roast poussins with sunshine saffron yogurt

A dish that adds a burst of sunshine to the table and requires very little of your time and attention, in fact just two lots of light blending. It is fabulous as it is, or with a salad and some potatoes or crusty bread on the side. Saffron is expensive. It adds its lovely musky flavour but, if you don't have any or if it isn't a special occasion, leave it out, the dish will still be great. You can use a whole chicken instead and cook it for 75–90 minutes, depending on its size.

Using a hand-held blender or a mini food processor, whizz all the marinade ingredients together until smooth. Pierce the poussins all over with a fork and ease off the skin over the breast. Rub the marinade all over the birds and under the skin of the breasts, too. Cover and marinate for at least one hour, or a couple if you have the time, in the fridge. Put the saffron for the yogurt (if using) in a cup or small bowl with the hot milk (if using) or 1 tbsp of hot water and set aside.

When ready to cook, return the poussins to room temperature and preheat the oven to 180°C/350°F/gas mark 4.

Place the poussins in a roasting tin and roast for 40–45 minutes or until cooked through, basting halfway. To check they're ready, pierce with a knife between the leg and the thigh and check if the juices run clear. If there is any trace of pink, continue to cook for five minutes before checking again. Take out of the oven, baste again with the pan juices and leave to rest, covered, for five minutes.

Meanwhile, mix together the mayonnaise, yogurt, garlic, lemon juice, coriander, most of the tomato, the infused saffron liquid and salt and pepper to taste.
If possible, leave to infuse for 10–15 minutes, to give the saffron's golden colour time to develop.

Serve the poussins whole or halved, drizzled with any remaining pan juices. Serve the sunshine yogurt on the side, sprinkled with some of the reserved tomatoes.

Serves 4

4 poussins

For the marinade
2 tbsp olive oil
8 tbsp Greek yogurt
8 fat garlic cloves, peeled
25g root ginger, peeled weight, coarsely chpped
3 tsp ground cumin
2–4 green chillies, deseeded if you prefer less heat
1 good tsp turmeric
2 tbsp lemon juice
2 tsp salt

For the sunshine saffron yogurt
good pinch of saffron (optional)
1 tbsp hot milk (optional)
3 good tbsp mayonnaise
225g Greek yogurt
1 largish garlic clove, or to taste, grated
½ tsp lemon juice
large handful of chopped coriander leaves and stalks
1 large ripe tomato, chopped
freshly ground black pepper

SLOW EASY COOK

One-pot meatballs, eggs and spiced tomatoes

This is a lovely meal. It is easy to make, even while helping the children with their homework, filling and very satisfying. You can use minced chicken instead of lamb, if you prefer. Serve with plain rice or Indian breads. It does take a little longer than some of the other dishes in the book, but is definitely worth having in your repertoire.

Start with the tomato sauce. Heat the vegetable oil in a large sauté pan that has a lid, add the onion and cook until golden brown. Add the garlic and cook for a further minute. Add the cumin and turmeric and stir for 20 seconds before adding the tomatoes, some salt and pepper and the sugar along with 50ml of water. Bring to the boil, then reduce the heat, cover and simmer for 15–20 minutes, or until the tomatoes are cooked. Taste, it should taste harmonious. Adjust the seasoning.

Meanwhile, mix together all the ingredients for the meatballs, seasoning generously with salt and pepper. Roll the mixture into balls slightly smaller than a walnut. Add them to the pan, cover and simmer for another 16–18 minutes, turning halfway.

Uncover the pan, adding a little water if it is looking dry. Make four little indents in the sauce and crack the eggs into them. Cover and simmer for another four to five minutes, or until the eggs are done to your liking. Taste, adjust the seasoning and serve with a sprinkling of coriander on top.

Serves 4

For the tomatoes and eggs
3 tbsp vegetable oil
1 onion, finely chopped
2 fat garlic cloves, grated
½ tsp ground cumin
¼ tsp turmeric
3 large ripe tomatoes (about 450g), chopped
salt and freshly ground black pepper
good pinch of caster sugar
4 eggs
handful of chopped coriander leaves, to serve

For the meatballs
250g minced lamb
15g chopped coriander leaves and stalks
2 garlic cloves, finely chopped
10g root ginger, peeled weight, finely chopped
½ tsp garam masala
½ tsp ground cumin

LUNCH
FOR FRIENDS

Herb and lemon paneer salad

This is a fresh and filling main course salad. Home-made paneer (see below) is tender, and easy and really satisfying to make (all you need is milk, lemon juice or yogurt, a saucepan and a sieve). If you don't want to make it, you can use buffalo mozzarella, feta, or, if you have store-bought paneer, put it in just-boiled water for 10 minutes to help soften it before using.

Blend together all the ingredients for the dressing until smooth and lightly emulsified. (I use a hand-held blender for this.)

Toss the dressing with the paneer, cucumber, radishes and onion and leave for five minutes or so. Toss in the leaves and nuts before serving with the avocado slices.

Serves 2 as a main or 4 as a side, can be doubled

For the dressing
4 tbsp extra virgin olive oil
1 small garlic clove, grated
2 tbsp lemon juice
$\frac{1}{4}$ tsp chaat masala
handful of mixed soft herbs (at least three, such as mint, dill, coriander, parsley, chives etc)
$\frac{1}{4}$ red chilli, finely chopped
1 tbsp crème fraîche (optional, but brings it all together)
1 rounded tsp Dijon mustard
good pinch of caster sugar

For the salad
200g paneer, ideally home-made (see left), sliced horizontally into thin shards or into cubes
100g cucumber, cut into long batons
100g radishes, thinly sliced
$\frac{1}{4}$ red onion, sliced
2 handfuls of baby salad leaves
small handful of honey-roast cashew nuts (or other nuts)
1 small avocado, sliced

make it better: *home-made paneer*

Bring 2 litres of whole milk to a boil in a heavy-based pan, stirring and scraping often to make sure it does not scorch. Boil for five minutes, then add the juice of 1 lemon (or 250g live yogurt). Stir while the mixture splits into curds and whey. Line a sieve with a muslin cloth or clean tea towel, place in the sink and pour in the contents of the pan. Tie the cloth into a bag over the curds and hang it from the kitchen tap. Allow to drip for 20 minutes. Now, still in its cloth bag, pat it out to a 2.5cm-thick disc and place on a board. Put the board in the kitchen sink and place a saucepan filled with water on top. Leave to drain for one or two hours for firm paneer, less for a softer curd. Store in water in the fridge and use up within two or three days. Before cooking, soak in just-boiled water for 10 minutes to soften. Makes 250g.

Rustic spiced spinach tart

A fun, easy tart that is a great way to enjoy Indian flavours. I admit it, this takes 30 minutes preparation, but, if you make the elements ahead of time, it needs only minutes to assemble before baking. I make my own pastry because I enjoy it, but it's quicker and easier to buy it ready-made, if you prefer (though it's nicest if you can find an all-butter version).

If you're making the pastry, cut the butter into the flour in a big bowl, using two forks; the butter will still be in large clumps. Add the salt and most of the water and continue to bring the dough together with a fork by stirring. Check if it is ready by taking a bit to see if it holds together in your hands. If so, very lightly bring the dough together into a ball (if not, add tiny splashes of water until it does). Flatten into a 10cm disc, wrap in cling film and place in the fridge for at least 30 minutes.

Meanwhile, blanch the spinach in a pot of boiling water until just wilted (a matter of seconds). Pour into a colander and rinse in cold water. Set aside. When cool enough to handle, squeeze it in your hands to remove as much water as possible.

Heat the oil and butter in a sauté pan. Add the onion and cook until softened and caramelising on the edges. Add the garlic and cook gently for another minute. Add the spices and stir well for a few minutes to cook through, then add the spinach, dill, lemon juice and some salt. Cook for another few minutes or until well mixed and dry. Taste and adjust the seasoning and lemon juice once more. Leave to cool.

When ready to cook, preheat the oven to 200°C/400°F/gas mark 6. Roll out the pastry on a piece of lightly floured baking parchment or greaseproof paper until it is about 25cm in diameter (or cut out a 25cm circle from a pre-rolled sheet). Spoon the spinach mixture evenly over the pastry, leaving a 3.5cm border, then scatter over the chilli and tomato. Pull up the sides of the pastry over the edges of the filling, without worrying about details, and place on a baking sheet. Bake in the oven for 35–40 minutes, or until lightly golden and crisp. Serve hot or warm.

Serves 4–5

For the pastry (optional, or use shop-bought shortcrust pastry)
90g chilled butter, cut into 2cm cubes
175g plain flour, plus more to dust
good pinch of salt
9 tbsp ice-cold water (I add ice cubes to a bowl of water)

For the filling
600g whole leaf or baby spinach, shredded if whole, washed
2 tbsp vegetable oil
25g unsalted butter
1 large onion, chopped
5 fat garlic cloves, chopped
1 rounded tsp ground cumin
1 rounded tsp ground coriander
30g dill fronds, chopped
4 tsp lemon juice, or to taste
1 large red chilli, finely sliced
1 smallish tomato, chopped

time-saving star: shop-bought pastry

BUNCH OF FRESH CURRY LEAVES

I find it astounding that curry leaves are not sold in every supermarket. Peppery, fragrant and aromatic, they enhance so many Indian (and South-east Asian) dishes. The dried leaves are no substitute so, when you find the fresh variety in Indian stores or large supermarkets, snap them up in bulk. They freeze brilliantly.

20-minute Indian west coastal baby squid

Score your squid and chop your onion. Think you can manage? This is a super-easy dish inspired by the flavours of the west coast of India. I use baby squid as it is very tender, but you can use bigger squid; it just takes another 30 seconds. A lovely summery dish, this is good with rice or crusty bread.

Slice the squid bodies in half lengthways and score gently on one side in a criss-cross pattern. Toss in ¼ tsp of the turmeric and ¼ tsp of salt. Set aside.

Heat 2 tbsp of the oil in a saucepan. Add half the curry leaves for 10 seconds, then the onion and green chillies; sauté until soft and colouring on the edges.

Add the garlic and ginger and sauté gently for one minute, until the garlic smells cooked. Add the tomatoes, spices (including the remaining ½ tsp of turmeric) and some salt. Add a splash of water and cook over a medium heat until the masala thickens and releases oil back into the pan, around 10 minutes. It should taste harmonious. Add 75ml of hot water and the lemon juice and take off the heat.

Heat the remaining oil in a large sauté pan until very hot, add the remaining curry leaves and follow with the squid. Sauté for 40 seconds in the hot oil, then add the masala, toss to coat well and cook for a further 30 seconds. Serve hot.

Serves 4

400g baby squid, cleaned
  by your fishmonger
¾ tsp turmeric
salt
3 tbsp coconut or vegetable oil
16–18 fresh curry leaves
1 onion, finely chopped
1–2 green chillies, pierced with
  the tip of a knife
4 large garlic cloves, grated
15g root ginger, peeled
  weight, grated
2 smallish tomatoes, blended
  until smooth
1 tsp freshly ground
  black pepper
⅔ tsp garam masala
1 rounded tsp ground
  fennel seeds
½ tsp ground cumin
1 tbsp lemon juice, or to taste

time-
saving star:
*shop-bought
tamarind
and date
chutney*

Quick-grilled pork with noodles and coconut broth

A multi-layered dish with sweet, lightly spiced pork, this uses a cheat's tamarind chutney which you can buy, or make my quick version (see page 155). The coconut broth is full of flavour and can be made ahead of time; I sometimes add a 5cm piece of creamed coconut for extra richness. You will need eight bamboo skewers.

Leave the bamboo skewers to soak in water for at least 30 minutes while you get on with the dish.

Stir together the marinade ingredients, adding 1 tsp of salt, until the sugar dissolves. Place the pork slices into a shallow dish. Add the marinade, turn to coat and leave to marinate while you make the broth.

Heat the oil for the broth in a large non-stick saucepan. Add the mustard seeds and, once the popping subsides, add the curry leaves, onion, pepper and some seasoning and cook on a medium-high flame until they are soft. Add the ginger and garlic and cook for one minute, stirring often and adding a splash of water if the garlic sticks. Add the chilli, coconut milk, stock and garam masala, bring to a boil, then reduce the heat and simmer for 10 minutes. Taste and adjust the salt, adding black pepper to taste.

While the broth simmers, preheat the grill and place a grill rack on the upper shelf. Thread the pork on to the drained skewers so that the slices lie flat (as in the photo), and grill for two or three minutes each side.

Meanwhile, cook the noodles according to the packet instructions and place straight into warmed bowls. Spoon over the broth, top with the coriander and the pork skewers and serve.

Serves 4

For the marinade
5 tbsp tamarind and date
  chutney (store-bought, or
  see page 155)
1 rounded tsp caster sugar
15g root ginger, peeled
  weight, grated
3–4 garlic cloves, grated
1 tbsp vegetable oil
salt and freshly ground
  black pepper

For the dish
1 large tenderloin of pork,
  cut into ¾–1cm slices on
  the diagonal
200g rice noodles
small handful of coriander leaves

For the coconut broth
3 tbsp vegetable oil
1 tsp mustard seeds
16–18 fresh curry leaves
1 large onion, sliced
1 small red pepper, finely sliced
25g root ginger, peeled weight,
  cut into julienne
4 fat garlic cloves, chopped
1 small red chilli, finely sliced
400ml coconut milk
400ml chicken stock
1 tsp garam masala

Mushrooms in a rich broth

Much lighter than a curry, this has the same depth of flavour, perfect for a lighter meal. You do need a variety of mushrooms for their different textures and tastes; I avoid button mushrooms as they have little of either. Serve this with Cumin and Smoked Almond Quinoa (see page 143) for a complete healthy meal, or simply with rice.

Start with the broth. Set the dried mushrooms to soak in 75ml just-boiled water while you cook. Heat the oil in a large non-stick saucepan. Add the peppercorns, cardamom and onion and cook on a high heat until well browned on the edges, then add the ginger and garlic, reduce the heat and cook, stirring, for 30–40 seconds. Add the tomato purée, shiitake mushrooms and some salt and cook for a few minutes to get some colour on them. Add the stock and soy sauce. Strain the dried mushrooms, reserving the soaking liquor, and add the mushrooms to the pan with most of their liquor, leaving behind the dregs. Bring to a boil, then reduce the heat and simmer for 30 minutes, or until the stock has reduced by half. Leave to cool a little, then strain through a sieve, pressing on the solids to ensure that you have drawn out all the moisture. Discard the solids and keep the stock.

Now for the spiced mushrooms. Heat the oil in a large, wide sauté pan. Add the red chillies and mustard seeds. Once the popping dies down, add the curry leaves and ginger and cook until the ginger has some colour. Add the mushrooms and a good pinch of salt and sauté until the mushrooms are golden and the water they release has dried up. Add the tomato, cumin and the mushroom broth and bring to a simmer. Season to taste with salt and black pepper and serve.

Serves 4

For the broth
20g dried mushrooms
2 tbsp vegetable oil
1 tbsp black peppercorns
2 black cardamom pods
  (optional)
1 large onion, sliced
20g root ginger, peeled weight,
  roughly chopped
4 fat garlic cloves,
  roughly chopped
2 tsp tomato purée
350g shiitake mushrooms
salt
1 litre vegetable stock or water
1 tbsp tamari or dark soy sauce

For the spiced mushrooms
2 tbsp vegetable oil
2 dried red chillies
$\frac{1}{2}$ tsp mustard seeds
12 fresh curry leaves
10g root ginger, peeled weight,
  cut into julienne
350g mixed mushrooms, sliced
  or torn into large pieces
  (oyster, chestnut and shiitake)
1 tomato, finely chopped
$\frac{3}{4}$ tsp ground cumin
freshly ground black pepper

Warm crispy duck and cape gooseberry salad

A really great warm salad to serve as a starter, a light main course or on a big platter for people to share with other salads and light meals. I love eating this way, sharing and taking as much or as little as I like from lots of different dishes.

Serves 4, can be doubled

For the salad
2 large duck breasts
salt and freshly ground
  black pepper
15cm piece of cucumber
1 smallish red onion,
  finely sliced
150g cape gooseberries
  (sometimes sold as physalis)
120g mixed salad leaves
  (I use a watercress, spinach
  and rocket combination)
2 large handfuls of honey-roast
  cashew nuts
handful of mint leaves

For the dressing
3 tbsp sherry vinegar
3 tbsp extra virgin olive oil
30g root ginger, peeled
  weight, grated
6 tsp runny honey

Preheat the oven to 180°C/350°F/gas mark 4. Trim off excess fat and skin from the edges of the duck breasts, then lightly score the remaining fat with a sharp knife. Season each well with salt and black pepper on the skin side. Turn and season only with salt on the flesh side. Place a large ovenproof non-stick frying pan on the hob. When it's very hot, add the breasts, skin-side down, then reduce the heat to its lowest setting. Cook undisturbed for eight minutes, or until golden and crisp, then turn and place in the oven for six to eight minutes, depending on size.

Meanwhile, cut the length of cucumber in half widthways, then halve both pieces again lengthways. Remove the seeds with a spoon, discard them, then slice the cucumber flesh into very slim batons, or julienne.

Whisk together all the dressing ingredients with 1½ tbsp of water and set aside.

Once the duck is cooked, place it on a plate to rest. Remove the excess fat from the pan, leaving behind about 1 tbsp. Return the pan to the heat and add the onion for one minute, seasoning lightly. Add the cape gooseberries and the dressing and cook for 40 seconds to warm through all the ingredients and deglaze the pan. Take off the heat, taste and adjust the seasoning.

When the duck has rested for five minutes, slice it thinly. Toss the remaining salad ingredients with the dressing and duck and serve.

Butternut, mushroom and crème fraîche filo tart

A special occasion tart that comes together easily, this looks very impressive despite needing no artistic skill at all, such is the forgiving nature of filo. The mushrooms provide an earthy, spicy element that contrasts well with the sweet squash, while the crème fraîche brings it all together. This is delicious in the summer as it is light and crispy, but also in autumn when squash is properly in season. It only needs a green salad to accompany it.

Preheat the oven to 220°C/425°F/gas mark 7. Place the squash in a baking tin and bake until soft, around 20 minutes. Remove from the oven and set aside.

Meanwhile, mix together all the ingredients for the marinade. Prepare the mushrooms: keep small shiitake and oyster mushrooms whole, but halve the others. Toss them in the marinade, making sure each piece is coated.

Place the coated mushrooms in a baking tray, trying to space them out so that they lie in a single layer. Bake alongside the squash for 15 minutes, turning halfway, or until the mushrooms have released their moisture and have started to sizzle in the remaining oil and colour on both sides. Remove the mushrooms from the oven.

Reduce the oven temperature to 190°C/375°F/gas mark 5 and place a baking tray on the centre shelf. Season the crème fraîche lightly and beat in the egg.

Meanwhile, butter a 20–22.5cm tart tin with a removeable base. Take one sheet of filo, generously brush it with melted butter and place over the base of the tin, leaving both sides overhanging. Repeat with the next filo sheet, placing at a right angle to the first to form a cross. Repeat with another three sheets, laying each at a different angle. Scatter the squash evenly over, then the mushrooms. Finally, pour over the crème fraîche mixture.

Bring in the edges of the pastry whilst roughly scrunching the ends (this will create lovely crispy bits). Brush the last two sheets of filo with butter, roughly scrunch them up and place over the exposed filling in the centre. Place the tart on the hot baking tray and bake for 40 minutes, or until the pastry is golden brown.

Remove and allow the tart to cool for five to 10 minutes or so before attempting to remove it from the tin. Serve hot or warm with a simple green salad.

Serves 6

For the tart
200g butternut squash, peeled and cut into 2cm cubes
300g shiitake, oyster and chestnut mushrooms, cleaned
salt and freshly ground black pepper
8 tbsp crème fraîche
1 egg
70g unsalted butter, melted, plus more for the tin
7 sheets filo pastry

For the tandoori marinade
1 large or 2 small garlic cloves, grated
8g root ginger, peeled weight, grated
¼ tsp chilli powder
¾ tsp garam masala
¾ tsp ground cumin
2 tbsp lemon juice
4 tbsp olive oil

Pistachio-crusted seared tuna salad

This is a special salad, memorably good to eat, easy to make and impressive to look at. It is the perfect lunch for entertaining. Great as a main course on a summer's day for friends, or make a large platter for a group to share with other dishes.

Grind the pistachios for the salad coarsely, so some bits are more powdery and others remain chunky and crunchy. Set aside.

Season the tuna on both sides.

Blend together all the ingredients for the dressing with 6 tbsp of water (I use a hand-held blender for this); taste and adjust the seasoning, adding a large pinch of freshly ground black pepper.

Take a large bowl and throw in the radishes, courgettes, fennel, herbs, lemon juice, cumin and chilli. Toss with the dressing to coat well.

Heat the oil in a large non-stick frying pan over a medium heat. Press the tuna into the ground pistachios to coat, turn and repeat on the other side. Add to the pan and cook undisturbed for one or two minutes, then turn over and cook for another one or two minutes, or until the tuna is cooked to your liking.

Toss the leaves into the dressing and vegetables in the bowl and divide the salad between four plates. Top each portion with the pistachio-crusted tuna and serve.

Serves 4

For the salad
90g shelled pistachios
salt and freshly ground
  black pepper
2 large tuna steaks, each cut in
  half to make 4 portions
200g radishes, finely sliced
2 smallish courgettes, sliced
  into ribbons using a
  vegetable peeler
1 largish fennel bulb,
  finely sliced
large handful of coriander
  leaves
small handful of mint leaves
juice of ½ lemon
large pinch of ground cumin
1 large red chilli, deseeded
  and chopped
1 tbsp vegetable oil
100g or so mixed baby leaves
  (around 1 handful per person)

For the pistachio dressing
90g shelled pistachios
9 tbsp olive oil
6 tbsp lemon juice
large pinch of caster sugar

Speedy spatchcocked quails

This is ridiculously easy. It takes minutes to make and cook (although, for the best results, leave to marinate for one hour). This will soon become your favourite quick meal and all it needs is salad or some rice and vegetables. Spatchcocking is very easy and essential in the repertoire of a time-saving cook, as the birds will be ready so much more quickly. Try these with Herby Quinoa and Chickpea Salad and a dollop of yogurt (see page 143), or Tamarind Chilli-glazed Sweet Potatoes (see page 141).

Spatchcock your quails: place a bird breast-side down on a work surface. Using kitchen scissors or poultry shears, cut down either side of the backbone all the way, to cut it out. Turn over and press down on the breastbone with the heel of your hand to gently flatten. Tuck the little legs slightly in and, taking one skewer (if using), pierce one leg at a diagonal angle through to the opposite wing. Repeat with the other side, through the other leg and wing, so the quail is speared with two diagonal skewers, as in the photo. This helps the bird keep its shape (but if you don't have any skewers the recipe will still work fine). Season both sides lightly. Repeat to spatchcock the remaining quails.

Mix together all the ingredients for the marinade and smear over the quail, coating both sides well. Cover and marinate in the fridge for one hour, or a couple of hours if you have time.

When ready to cook, preheat the grill (I use an oven grill and the fan). Place the quails on an oiled baking tray or foil on the middle shelf. Cook for eight minutes, then turn and cook for another four or five minutes or until done and golden on both sides. Check the birds are cooked by piercing the largest through its thickest point; the juice should run clear with no trace of pink. If they are not ready, cook for a few minutes longer, then check again. Serve immediately.

Makes 4, can be doubled

For the quails
4 quails, spatchcocked (ask your butcher or see recipe, it's very easy)
8 bamboo skewers (optional)
salt and freshly ground black pepper
vegetable oil, for the tray

For the marinade
½ red onion, finely chopped
12g root ginger, peeled weight, grated
5 fat garlic cloves, grated
½ tsp ground cinnamon
2 scant tsp ground cumin
2 scant tsp garam masala
½ tsp chilli powder
200g plain yogurt
½ tsp salt
2 big pinches of black pepper
lemon juice

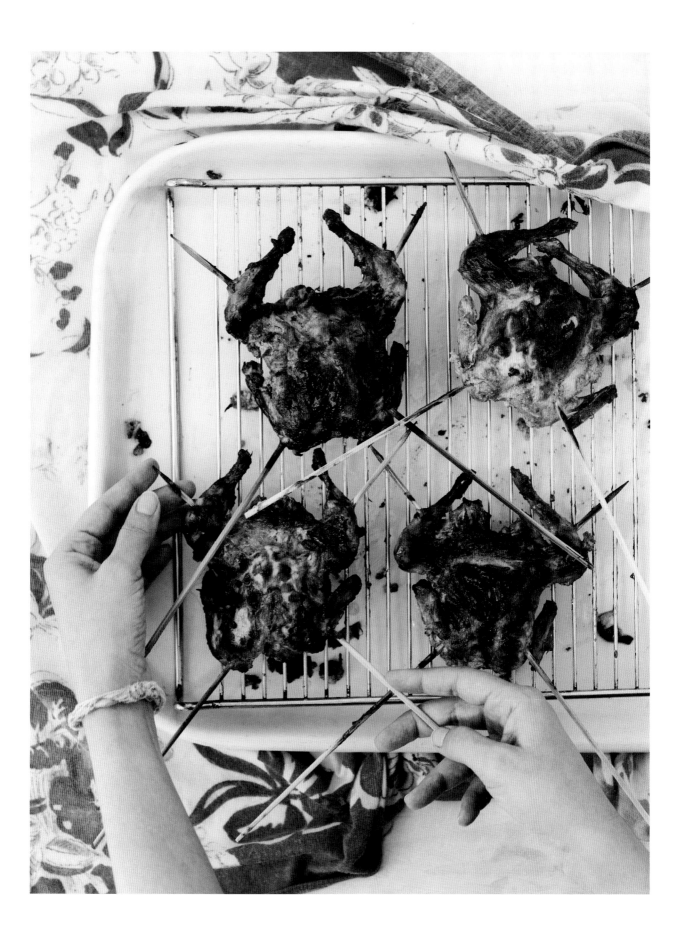

AFTER WORK

Super-healthy sprouted mung chaat with crispy spinach

This is a surprisingly tasty salad that I serve to friends and eat by myself for a light meal, as it is so satisfying, almost in spite of being so nutritious! It is also fantastic with 10-minute Spiced Lamb Chops (see page 84) or with a simply grilled steak. You can buy the tamarind chutney in Indian markets or online (I love the Maggi brand) and the coriander chutney whizzes together in seconds, but, if you don't have the ingredients for that, just add a little lemon juice and a bit more coriander. I bake the spinach until crispy – and it is a revelation – but once mixed in a salad it needs to be eaten quickly or it becomes soggy. If baking the spinach is a step too far, just add some raw baby spinach to the salad, or leave it out.

Preheat the oven to 160°C/325°F/gas mark 3.

Put the spinach leaves in a large bowl, add the oil and toss with your hands to coat all the leaves. Place on one or two large baking trays, as near as possible in a single layer. Season lightly with salt and bake for 25 minutes, or until the leaves are crisp. Take out of the oven and set aside.

Meanwhile, boil the sprouted beans in water for six to eight minutes, or until al dente but not crunchy. Drain. Add the tomato, onion, coriander and coriander chutney; taste and season with salt if you like.

Mix the yogurt with the roasted ground cumin, taste and adjust the seasoning.

When you are ready to eat, spoon the yogurt on to serving plates. Mound the sprouted bean mixture on top, drizzle well with the tamarind chutney, then arrange over the crisp spinach. Sprinkle over the peanuts (if using), then serve immediately.

Serves 2 as a light meal, or 4 as a side

2 handfuls baby spinach leaves, well washed, left to dry on kitchen paper
2–3 tbsp vegetable oil
salt
200g mixed sprouted beans
1 largish tomato, finely chopped
1 small red onion, finely chopped
large handful of chopped coriander leaves
6 tbsp Tangy Coriander Chutney (see page 154)
250g Greek yogurt
⅓ tsp roasted ground cumin (see page 92)
120–135ml tamarind chutney (store bought or home-made, see page 155)
handful of roasted salted peanuts, chopped (optional)

time-saving star: *shop-bought tamarind and date chutney*

Creamy mustard no-fuss fish

A lovely, light but full-flavoured dish inspired by the flavours of Bengal. I think this is perfect just served with some vegetables; try Edgy Peas (see page 144) or Potatoes Sautéed with Dill (see page 139). I like the spice of the chillies in this recipe, but you can leave them out if you prefer. If you can find mustard oil, it will add a lot of flavour.

Season the fish on both sides.

Heat half the oil in a large non-stick sauté pan. (If using mustard oil, heat until it comes to smoking point, then cool for 30 seconds.) Add the dried chillies, mustard and nigella seeds and cook until the popping starts to die down. Add the onion, green chillies and some salt and cook until the onion is soft and just starting to colour on the edges.

Add the garlic and cook over a gentle flame until it is cooked, around one minute, then add the ground coriander and turmeric with a small splash of water and cook for two to three minutes. Add the mustard, cream and 200ml of water and bring to the boil. Cook for five minutes for the flavours to come together. Add the lemon juice, taste and adjust the seasoning. Pour into a bowl and place the coriander on top of the mustard sauce. Give the sauté pan a wipe.

Add the remaining oil to the pan and heat until quite hot. (Again, if using mustard oil, heat until it comes to smoking point, then cool for 30 seconds.) Place over a high heat. Pat the fish dry with kitchen paper and add it to the pan, skin-side down. Cook for 30 seconds, then reduce the heat. Cook for another minute, or until the skin is crisp. Carefully flip over and add the mustard sauce. The sauce should come at least one-quarter of the way up the side of the fillets; if not, add a splash of water from the kettle. Simmer gently for two or three minutes, or until the fish is cooked through. Taste, adjust the seasoning and lemon juice and serve.

Serves 4

salt and a good grinding of freshly ground black pepper
4 x 150g fillets of firm white fish
4 tbsp pure mustard oil or other vegetable oil
1–2 dried chillies (optional)
½ tsp brown mustard seeds
½ tsp nigella seeds
1 onion, finely sliced
1–2 green chillies, pierced with the tip of a knife (optional)
5 fat garlic cloves, grated
1 tbsp ground coriander
½ tsp turmeric
1 rounded tsp English mustard
50ml double cream
2–3 tsp lemon juice, or to taste
handful of chopped coriander leaves

Parsi coconut cod parcels "special delivery"

This is another really easy dish which takes minutes to put together and another 10 minutes or so to cook. Traditionally the parcels were made from banana leaves, which impart an additional flavour, but I usually bake them in foil as here. If you live near a seller of banana leaves, go all out and use them. These can be steamed, baked or fried (in banana leaves, for five minutes on each side). Serve with a simple pilaf, vegetables or a salad.

Preheat the oven to 180°C/350°F/gas mark 4.

Using a hand-held blender, whizz together the garlic, lemon juice, oil or butter, sugar, herbs, chillies and spices until smooth. Add the coconut and mix well. Taste and adjust the seasoning, also lightly seasoning the fish on both sides.

Coat the fish pieces well in the spice paste on both sides. Place each fillet on a piece of foil (or a banana leaf) and fold to make a loose envelope, ensuring the parcels are sealed and won't leak while cooking.

Bake in the oven for 10–15 minutes depending on thickness. Serve hot.

Serves 4

5 fat garlic cloves
3 tbsp lemon juice
1 tbsp vegetable oil or
  melted butter
1¾ tsp caster sugar
25g coriander leaves, stalks
  and roots, well washed
1–2 green chillies
1 rounded tsp ground cumin
2½ tsp ground coriander
50g finely grated fresh coconut
  (I use defrosted frozen
  coconut, see page 9)
salt and freshly ground
  black pepper
4 large cod fillets

time-
saving star:
*frozen grated
coconut*

Indian stir-fried spring veg vermicelli with peanuts

Vermicelli and rice noodles feature on Indian menus, the former in desserts in North India as well as in quick stir-fries in many regions, the latter mostly in the South. This recipe is inspired by those northern vegetable stir-fries. If you make the recipe with fine vermicelli (available in Indian stores), you will produce a softer, more unctuous dish. Rice noodles, used here, are more textured but also more widely available. Both work well. I like to add edamame beans for a little protein, but you can use broad beans or peas for a burst of sweetness if you prefer. I like to serve it with a little Coastal Coconut Chutney on the side (see page 154).

Heat the oil in a large non-stick sauté pan. Add the chillies and mustard seeds and, once the popping dies down, the chana dal and curry leaves. Once the lentils start to colour, add the red onion, ginger and seasoning and sauté for three to four minutes before adding the turmeric. Fry for 20 seconds, stirring to mix well, then add the rest of the vegetables.

Stir-fry for two minutes, then add the rice noodles and lemon juice and continue to cook for another two minutes, or until the noodles are soft but the vegetables are still crunchy. Stir in the herbs and peanuts and serve hot or warm.

Serves 2

2–3 tbsp vegetable oil
2 dried red chillies
1 tsp brown mustard seeds
2 tsp *chana dal*
14 fresh curry leaves
1 red onion, finely sliced
15g root ginger, peeled weight, finely shredded
salt and freshly ground black pepper
¼ tsp turmeric
1 large carrot, cut into 7.5cm matchsticks
12 asparagus spears, tips cut whole on the diagonal, stalks finely sliced
2 spring onions, finely sliced on the diagonal
2 handfuls of edamame beans
300g packet fine rice noodles
2–3 tbsp lemon juice, to taste
small handful of finely chopped mint or coriander leaves
small handful of roasted salted peanuts, lightly crushed

10 mins to cook

Crispy fish with creamy caper chutney

So speedy and simple that you will return to this recipe again and again. The fish is moist, the semolina crunchy and the chutney adds herby, tangy, creamy contrast. I serve this with a side salad or vegetables for a light meal, but it also makes an amazing fried fish sandwich with some lettuce leaves and tomato slices.

Start with the fish. In a wide bowl, mix the turmeric, olive oil, ½ tsp of salt and some black pepper, the lemon zest and juice and garlic. Score the skin side of each fish fillet with three shallow slashes, then place in the marinade and massage well on both sides. Leave to marinate for 20 minutes while you make the chutney.

For the chutney, blend together most of the coriander and mint with the chilli, pistachios, lemon juice, crème fraîche and half the capers until smooth. (I use a hand-held blender.) Chop the remaining herbs and stir them in with the remaining capers and the mayonnaise. Taste and adjust the seasoning.

Season the semolina with ¼ tsp each of salt and pepper and place on a large baking tray or plate.

Heat the vegetable oil in a large, wide non-stick frying pan over a high heat (if you don't have a large pan, cook in two batches). Coat the fish in the semolina well on both sides and place in the hot oil, skin-side down. Reduce the heat to medium and cook for three minutes until golden and crispy, then carefully flip over and cook for another one or two minutes, depending on thickness.

Serve the fish with a good spoonful of the creamy caper chutney on the side.

Serves 4

For the fish
½ tsp turmeric
1½ tbsp olive oil
salt and freshly ground
  black pepper
finely grated zest of 1 unwaxed
  lemon plus 3 tsp lemon juice
1 fat garlic clove, grated
4 sea bream or sea bass fillets
120g coarse-grained semolina
4–5 tbsp vegetable oil

For the chutney
30g coriander leaves and
  stalks, well washed
20g mint leaves, well washed
1 green chilli, stalk removed,
  deseeded if you like less heat
30 pistachios (roasted if they're
  easier to find)
2 tsp lemon juice
3 tbsp crème fraîche
  (half-fat, if you prefer)
2½ tbsp capers (ideally baby
  capers), drained and rinsed
2 rounded tbsp mayonnaise

Tangy near-instant prawn curry

A lovely, creamy curry with the intense, rounded flavour of sun-dried tomatoes, which works so well with prawns. This is great with crusty bread, Indian breads, rice or even pasta! Provided you have gathered your ingredients to hand, you can start the curry when you put on the water to boil for the rice or pasta, and both should be ready at the same time.

Heat the oil in a large non-stick saucepan. Add the mustard seeds and, once the popping subsides, add the curry leaves. Follow quickly with the garlic and cook for one minute, or until the garlic smells cooked.

Add the tomatoes, tomato purée, ground spices and some salt and cook, stirring occasionally, until the masala has released oil on the base of the pan.

Add the prawns, crème fraîche and a good splash of water and simmer until the prawns are cooked through, a matter of three to four minutes. Taste and adjust the seasoning, stir in the coriander and serve hot.

Serves 4

2–3 tbsp vegetable oil
1 tsp mustard seeds
8–10 fresh curry leaves
3 fat garlic cloves, grated
2 large tomatoes, finely
  chopped or blended
4 tbsp sun-dried tomato purée,
  or to taste
½ tsp chilli powder
1 tsp garam masala
½ tsp turmeric
1 tsp ground coriander
½ tsp roasted ground cumin
  (see page 92)
salt
500g raw king prawns, shelled
  and deveined
3 tbsp crème fraîche,
  or single cream
large handful of chopped
  coriander leaves

FRESH CHORIZO

The Portuguese ruled Goa for more than 450 years. During this time, the local cuisine was influenced by the Portuguese diet, while the chorizo sausage the invaders brought with them took on a spicier incarnation in the subcontinent. It is hard to find hot Indian chorizo in this country, so I buy the regular fresh Portuguese or Spanish chorizo from my local deli and it works really well.

Goan chicken and chorizo stew

After a five-minute flurry of chopping and sautéing, you can leave this to cook itself. And there's only one pan to wash up. Serve it with toasted crusty bread to mop up the juices or, if you have more time, with Goan Tomato Rice or Goan Coconut Rice (see pages 80 and 130, though make the latter without the chorizo!).

Heat the oil in a non-stick saucepan and add the chorizo. Cook gently on both sides until the slices release their oil into the pan. Remove with a slotted spoon or fork and set aside.

Add the onion and cook for six to seven minutes, or until soft and golden on the edges. Add the ginger, garlic and chillies and cook for one minute until the garlic smells cooked, adding a splash of hot water from the kettle if it starts to stick.

Add all the ground spices, seasoning and a small splash of water and cook for 40–50 seconds. Stir in the flour and, after a minute or so, add the chicken and stock or water and return the chorizo. Bring to the boil, cover and simmer for 25 minutes or until the joints are cooked through: pierce the largest chicken thigh at its thickest point, the juices should run clear. If not, cook for a few minutes longer, then check again. Uncover after 20 minutes and cook off excess liquid if it is a little thin, or add water from the kettle if it is a bit too thick.

Add the tamarind solution, taste and adjust the seasoning. I like to take the meat off the bone and stir it back in, but I leave that up to you. Serve hot.

Serves 4–6

2 tbsp vegetable oil
4 links fresh chorizo sausages (mine are 7.5–10cm each), sliced
1 large onion, finely chopped
15g root ginger, peeled weight, grated
4 large garlic cloves, grated
1–2 green chillies, pierced with the tip of a knife
$1\frac{1}{2}$ tsp ground coriander
1 tsp garam masala, or to taste
1 tsp ground cumin
salt and freshly ground black pepper
1 rounded tbsp plain flour
6 large skinless bone-in chicken thighs, trimmed of excess fat
250ml chicken stock or water
$\frac{1}{4}$–$\frac{1}{2}$ tsp tamarind paste, to taste, dissolved in hot water

Chorizo with white beans and greens

A typical Goan dish that is very satisfying and great to come home to in cold weather. You have protein, carbs and greens all in one pot and it only takes minutes to make. This dish really reminds me of some Brazilian bean dishes that the Portuguese probably loved, kept and brought to Goa. It is now very much Goan soul food. Serve with crusty bread or some rice.

Heat the oil in a medium-large non-stick saucepan and add the sausages, colour on all sides, then remove with a slotted spoon and set aside. Add the onions to the flavoured oil and cook until golden brown on the edges. Add the garlic and cook for one minute, or until it smells cooked, adding a little water from the kettle if it sticks. Add the tomato purée and cook out for one or two minutes.

Return the sausages to the pan, then pour in the stock and enough water to cover. Leave to cook for 20 minutes, giving the pot an occasional stir.

Add the beans and greens and cook for four or five minutes, or until the greens are cooked through and the beans hot. There should be enough water for a brothy sauce, so add extra if necessary. Taste, adjust the seasoning and, once the greens have wilted, serve in warmed bowls.

Serves 4

2 tbsp vegetable oil
6 fresh chorizo sausages
2 smallish onions, sliced
4 fat garlic cloves, grated
2 tsp tomato purée
300ml chicken stock
400g can white beans, drained
  and rinsed
2–3 large handfuls of shredded
  greens (I use cavolo nero with
  the coarse ribs trimmed out)
salt and freshly ground
  black pepper

Goan tomato rice

This moist, flavourful dish is a staple in Goa. The spicy, smoky deliciousness of the chorizo makes it more of a special occasion main course and one that is hard to resist, but, if you leave the sausage out, the dish will still be wonderful as well as simple enough not to overpower whatever you pair it with.

Heat the oil in a non-stick pan. Add the whole spices and cook for 20–30 seconds. Tip in the onion and cook until soft and colouring at the edges, then add the chorizo and cook until the fat runs into the pan. Add the garlic and cook for another minute, or until it smells cooked.

Add the tomatoes, tomato purée, some salt and a splash of water. Cook over a medium-high flame until the tomatoes are cooked and the mixture has completely reduced and thickened, around 10–15 minutes. Add the rice, stir it into the tomatoes and cook for two minutes.

Pour in the stock. Stir well to mix, then taste the water and adjust the seasoning (see page 133), adding chilli powder to taste. Leave to boil for a few minutes, then reduce the heat to its lowest setting, cover and cook, undisturbed, for eight to 10 minutes. Check after eight minutes. When the grain is cooked and soft, turn off the heat and allow to steam, with the lid on, for another five to 10 minutes. Serve hot.

Serves 3–4

3 tbsp vegetable oil
6 cloves
5 green cardamom pods
5cm cinnamon stick
1 large onion, chopped
2 fresh chorizo sausages, sliced
2 fat garlic cloves, grated
2 tomatoes, blended or skinned
  and chopped
1 tbsp tomato purée
salt
200g basmati or other
  long-grain rice, washed well
  (see page 130)
400ml chicken stock
$\frac{1}{4}$–$\frac{1}{2}$ tsp chilli powder

Shredded ginger chicken

This is a typical midweek meal, easy but very tasty. It uses chicken without the bones in, so it is quicker to cook, but, if you have the time, buy chicken on the bone for added flavour and depth and cook it for about 25 minutes. Serve with Indian breads and raita on the side.

Heat the oil in a large saucepan. Add the onion and stir-fry for four or five minutes. Add the julienned ginger and continue cooking until it starts to colour. Add the grated ginger and garlic with a small splash of water and cook for a minute, or until the garlic smells cooked.

Meanwhile, blend together the tomatoes, yogurt, seasoning and ground spices until smooth (I use a hand-held blender). Add to the pan and bring to a boil, then reduce the heat and simmer until it has completely reduced and thickened, stirring often. Brown this paste for a further few minutes. It should taste harmonious.

Add the chicken, stock and vinegar. Bring to a boil and simmer, uncovered, until the chicken is cooked and most of the liquid has evaporated, five or six minutes, stirring occasionally. Check the chicken is cooked all the way through: pierce a large piece to its centre, the juices should run clear. If there is any trace of pink, cook for a couple of minutes more, then test again. Stir in the coriander, taste, adjust the seasoning and serve. It should not be a very watery curry, but you should have enough lovely juices to mop up with your bread.

Serves 3–4, can be doubled

4 tbsp vegetable oil
1 largish onion, finely chopped
30g root ginger, peeled weight, half julienned and half grated
4 fat garlic cloves, grated
2 ripe tomatoes, quartered
4 tbsp plain yogurt
salt and freshly ground black pepper
$3/4$–1 tsp garam masala
1 tsp ground coriander
1 tsp ground cumin
$1/2$ tsp chilli powder, or to taste
6 large skinless boneless chicken thighs, cut into large cubes
150ml chicken stock or water
1–2 tsp red wine vinegar, or to taste (optional)
handful of chopped coriander leaves

Easiest ever chicken pilaf

Sometimes, you just want everything thrown into one pot. This is that kind of recipe and perfect for a midweek family meal. I prefer chicken thighs as they have more flavour and succulence, but use breasts if you prefer. Lovely just as it is, with some yogurt on the side.

Wash the rice, then leave it to soak while you cook.

Heat the ghee or oil in a non-stick saucepan and add the cumin seeds. Once these have darkened, add the onions and fry over a medium heat until turning golden at the edges. Add the ginger and garlic, reduce the heat and cook for one minute, adding a splash of water if the garlic sticks.

Add the yogurt, chilli, turmeric, garam masala, some salt and black pepper. Cook over a high heat, stirring constantly, until it comes to a boil. Continue to cook, still stirring, for another three minutes, then add the chicken and cook until most of the yogurt has been absorbed and the masala releases oil back into the pan.

Drain the rice and stir it in with the stock. Taste the water and adjust the seasoning (see page 133). Bring to a boil, cover and reduce the heat to as low as it goes. Cook undisturbed for eight minutes, then check a grain of rice: it should be cooked. If not, cook for another minute or so. Turn off the heat and leave to steam for five minutes, with the lid on, or until you are ready to eat. Fork in a good squeeze of lemon juice and the spring onions and coriander (if using), fluffing up the rice as you do so, then serve.

Serves 4

300g basmati rice, washed well (see page 130)
2 tbsp ghee or vegetable oil
2 tsp cumin seeds
2 smallish onions, sliced
10g root ginger, peeled weight, grated
3 garlic cloves, grated
200g plain yogurt
½ tsp chilli powder, or to taste (optional)
½ tsp turmeric
1 rounded tsp garam masala
salt and a good grinding of freshly ground black pepper
400g skinless boneless chicken thighs, cut into large pieces
500ml chicken stock
½ lemon
2 spring onions, finely sliced
handful of coriander leaves, to serve (optional)

10-minute spiced lamb chops

These are lovely for a barbecue; just put them in the fridge to marinate the morning before you need them. Small, delicate cutlets make great appetisers with Tangy Coriander Chutney on the side (see page 154), or larger chops work as a main meal with vegetables or salad, naan and raita. If you don't have black cumin, use regular ground cumin instead.

Blend together all the ingredients for the marinade until smooth using a hand-held blender, adding enough salt for it to taste slightly salty to your palate.

Pierce the lamb all over with a fork and place in a shallow dish with the marinade, turning to coat well. Cover and marinate in the fridge for around two hours, or overnight if possible.

When ready to eat, preheat your oven to its highest temperature, or turn on the grill in the oven to its highest setting. Place the lamb on a baking tray and cook for nine to 10 minutes, turning halfway. Remove from the oven, cover and leave to rest for five minutes. Serve hot, with lemon wedges.

Makes 6, can be doubled

For the marinade
20g root ginger, peeled weight, coarsely chopped
5 fat garlic cloves
50g Greek yogurt
¼ tsp freshly ground black pepper
1 rounded tsp black cumin seeds (*shahi jeera*), or regular cumin seeds
¾ tsp chilli powder
1 tbsp garam masala
1¾ tbsp lemon juice
1 tbsp vegetable oil
salt

For the lamb
6 lamb chops or cutlets on the bone (remove all the fat)
lemon wedges, to serve

make it better: *tenderise with green papaya*

In India, cooks tenderise their meat with green papaya paste. Green papaya can be found in Oriental supermarkets so, if you find it, buy it and use on all your meats before using in a recipe. For the recipe above, grate 20g of green papaya and marinate the meat in this paste for 30 minutes, before wiping it off. Continue from the point of adding the spiced marinade.

Stir-fried coconut beef

A truly delicious dish from Kerala, this has a depth of flavour that belies its quick cooking time. It is sweet from the coconut, spiced and slightly hot. You can also add some vegetables such as green beans or mangetout; stir-fry those separately before adding them to the final dish. Like many stir-fries, this has several stages, but it's still easy. Serve with Indian breads, or with a simple pilaf and some yogurt.

Heat a large sauté pan. Add the coconut and lightly toast until golden, around two minutes, shaking the pan often. Pour into a large bowl and give the pan a wipe.

Add 1 tbsp of the oil to the pan and add the beef; sear quickly on all sides or until browned in spots. Tip straight on to the coconut.

Heat the remaining oil in the pan (no need to wipe it this time) and add the mustard seeds, cooking until the popping subsides. Add the curry leaves, onions and some salt and cook until browned on the edges. Add the ginger and garlic and stir-fry until the garlic is cooked through, about one minute.

Add the spices and give the pan a good stir. Add a good splash of water, the beef stock gel and tomato purée and cook for four or five minutes, or until the sauce is thick once more and beautifully glossy.

Return the beef to the pan with a splash of water and the coconut and stir well in the sauce. Cook for a few minutes until the sauce coats the beef, then serve.

Serves 4–6

60g desiccated coconut
4 tbsp vegetable oil
600g beef sirloin, fat removed, thinly sliced across the grain
$1\frac{1}{2}$ tsp mustard seeds
15 fresh curry leaves
2 small onions, finely chopped
salt
30g root ginger, finely julienned
6 large garlic cloves, chopped
$1\frac{1}{2}$ tsp freshly ground black pepper
$1\frac{1}{2}$ tbsp ground fennel seeds
3 tsp ground coriander
$1\frac{1}{2}$ tsp garam masala
$\frac{3}{4}$ tsp ground cumin
1 beef stock gel
2 rounded tbsp tomato purée

Easy 25-minute cardamom lamb

A lovely, light lamb curry inspired by Sindhi cardamom chicken curries. The flavours are delicate but quite wonderful and it cooks in less than 30 minutes. I truly recommend it. For quickest results, cook the curry in an open, wide pan so that there is more surface area for the ingredients to cook. If you have more time, make a slow-cooked version with cubed leg of lamb, cooking it for 1–1¼ hours for an added depth of flavour.

Blend together the yogurt, tomato, ginger, garlic and ground spices until smooth. (I use a hand-held blender.)

Heat the oil in a saucepan, add the onion and sauté until golden brown. Add the blended ingredients and the chillies and cook, stirring often, until the masala has completely reduced and releases oil on the base of the pan. The more you fry this paste mixture, the deeper the resulting flavour, so it is a time-versus-flavour decision. Add the stock and bring to the boil, then add the meat and simmer for four to five minutes, or until cooked to your liking.

Taste and add salt, pepper or more ground cardamom until you have a flavour you love, then serve.

Serves 3, can be doubled

1½ tbsp plain yogurt
1 smallish tomato, quartered
10g root ginger, peeled weight, coarsely chopped
2 fat garlic cloves
1 rounded tsp ground coriander
1 tsp ground cardamom, or to taste
1 tsp ground cumin
3 tbsp vegetable oil
1 onion, finely chopped
1–2 green chillies, pierced with the tip of a knife
200ml lamb or chicken stock, or water
350g lamb rump, trimmed and cut into 2.5cm chunks
salt and ½ tsp freshly ground black pepper

30-MINUTE SUPPERS

Parsi poached eggs on potatoes

Parsis have a love both of eggs and potatoes, so it is no surprise that this is one of their most popular dishes. It is one of my favourite ways to eat eggs; the combination just works. This can make a great brunch dish, of course, but I like it as a filling lunch or light supper with some vegetables on the side. You can serve it as it is, or with griddled bread or parathas.

Heat the oil in a large non-stick sauté pan that has a lid. Add the cumin seeds and, once they darken slightly and smell aromatic, add the onion. Sauté for five or six minutes, or until soft and starting to brown on the edges. Add the garlic, chilli and some salt and cook for a minute.

Add the spices and potatoes and stir well in the oil and onions. Add a splash of water, bring to the boil, cover and cook over a gentle heat for 12–14 minutes. Uncover to cook off all the extra moisture and allow the potatoes to colour as they finish cooking, another five to seven minutes or so. Taste and adjust the seasoning, adding black pepper to taste.

Stir in the coriander leaves and make four little hollows in the mixture with a spoon. Break the eggs into the hollows one at a time. Cover the pan and cook for three to five minutes, or until the whites are set but the yolks still molten. Sprinkle some salt and pepper or chilli powder (if using) over the eggs and serve hot.

Serves 2, can easily be doubled

2 tbsp vegetable oil
1 tsp cumin seeds
1 small red onion, finely sliced
2 fat garlic cloves, chopped
1 green chilli, finely chopped
salt and freshly ground
  black pepper
½ tsp ground coriander
⅓ tsp turmeric
2 smallish waxy potatoes
  (around 250g), halved
  and thinly sliced
small handful of chopped
  coriander leaves
4 eggs
chilli powder (optional)

Warm farro, lentil and courgette 'salad'

This was inspired both by *khichri*, a one-pot dish made with lentils and rice and lightly spiced with fried cumin seeds, as well as by a lentil salad I often make. It is a really simple, healthy-yet-filling dish. The farro is nutty and has a lovely texture, the lentils deliver a burst of earthy protein and the griddled courgettes add a charred flavour as well as sweet freshness. My farro cooks in 16–18 minutes, so I can cook it with the lentils, but the cooking time will vary between brands, so check the packet. If necessary, boil the farro separately and stir in at the end. This latter method will also give you a cleaner-looking finish.

Heat the oil in a non-stick saucepan. Add the onion and cook until golden brown. Add the lentils and farro with 750ml of water and the vegetable bouillon powder (if using) and bring to the boil. Simmer for around 18 minutes, or until both lentils and farro are cooked. Towards the end the water should nearly have evaporated, so you need to give it the occasional stir to stop anything burning. You want to drive off the excess water, so don't add any extra unless necessary.

Meanwhile, heat a large griddle pan, place the courgette slices in it and griddle until lightly charred on both sides. Set aside. When the lentils are done, stir in the remaining ingredients, mix well, season and serve warm.

Serves 2 generously

4 tbsp extra virgin olive oil
1 smallish onion,
  finely chopped
75g Puy lentils
150g farro
$\frac{1}{3}$ tsp vegetable bouillon
  powder (optional)
1 small courgette, finely sliced
$1\frac{1}{2}$ tsp each ground cumin and
  roasted ground cumin
  (see below left)
small handful of walnut pieces
1 rounded tbsp finely sliced red
  chilli, or to taste
good squeeze of lemon juice
large handful of mixed baby
  salad leaves
salt and freshly ground
  black pepper

make it better: *roast whole spices*

Tip the spices into a dry frying pan placed over a medium heat. Shake or stir often so they brown evenly. (Do not use a non-stick pan, as it may smoke and some believe this to be unhealthy.) When the spices colour and become aromatic – a matter of minutes – remove them from the heat and immediately pour into a mortar or a bowl to arrest the cooking; if you leave them in the pan, even off the heat, they may burn. Grind in a mortar and pestle, or a spice grinder, if needed.

Crispy Goan-spiced mackerel

This dish has fame beyond the sandy beaches and borders of Goa, because it is truly wonderful. My version is semi-easy as it requires the onion to be part-charred before blending with the remaining ingredients. If this is one step too far, add a larger pinch of sugar to the mix and leave the onion out. Serve with a salad or some vegetables.

Place the onion directly on a low flame, or in a griddle pan over a low heat, to char the outside layers; it will take about 10 minutes. Keep turning it and keep an eye on it (don't leave the kitchen!).

Blend together the garlic, ginger, spices, seasoning, vinegar, sugar and onion (removing the very charred outer bits) until you have a smooth paste. I use a hand-held blender for this.

Slash each side of the fish three times on the diagonal, to help the flavours penetrate the flesh. Place the semolina on a large plate.

Divide the onion paste into four. Open a fish out and smear most of one part of the paste on the inside, then fold back over to close and smear the rest on the outside. Repeat to coat the remaining fish in the remaining paste. Place each fish into the semolina, one by one, to coat both sides well.

Heat the oil in a non-stick frying pan large enough to accommodate all the fish. Once the oil is quite hot, add the fish, then reduce the heat. Cook without disturbing for four minutes, then turn the fish carefully and cook for another three or four minutes, or until crispy and golden on both sides.

Makes 4, can be doubled

1 small red onion, loose, papery outer skin removed
6 fat garlic cloves
10g root ginger, peeled weight, coarsely chopped
2 level tsp ground cumin
½ tsp turmeric
¾ tsp chilli powder
1 tsp garam masala
1 tsp salt and a good pinch of freshly ground black pepper
2 tbsp red or white wine vinegar
1 tsp caster sugar
4 medium mackerel, cleaned and butterflied by the fishmonger
8 tbsp semolina
6–7 tbsp vegetable oil

Smoked trout with kedgeree pilaf

A pilaf version of the famous Anglo-Indian brunch dish. The Memsahibs of the Raj adapted kedgeree from a very basic rice and lentil dish, *khichri*, incorporating their beloved smoked fish and eggs. It is delicious, comforting and a great midweek dinner. This is a lightly buttery and gently spiced version. I like a fried egg on top, but boil and quarter them if you prefer.

Heat the oil in a large non-stick saucepan. Add the cumin seeds and, once they darken, add the butter and onion. Sweat until the onion is soft but without colour. Add the garlic and cook for one minute, or until it smells cooked.

Add the spices to the onion pan with some seasoning and cook for 30–40 seconds. Add the drained rice and stir to coat in the flavourings, then pour in 600ml of water. Bring to the boil and allow to bubble for a minute, then reduce the heat to its lowest and cover the pot with a lid.

Cook for seven to eight minutes, then check a grain of rice. If it is cooked, turn off the flame, place the trout on top to warm through, cover and leave the rice to steam for five minutes or so.

Meanwhile, heat a little oil in a large frying pan and fry your eggs as you like them.

Gently stir the lemon juice, trout and parsley into the rice, using a fork and leaving the trout in large flakes. Serve portions topped with a fried egg.

Serves 4

2 tsp vegetable oil, plus more
  for the eggs
1$\frac{1}{2}$ tsp cumin seeds
50g butter
1 largish onion, finely chopped
4 fat garlic cloves, chopped
$\frac{3}{4}$ tsp turmeric
2 tsp ground coriander
1 tsp garam masala
salt and lots of freshly ground
  black pepper
300g basmati rice, washed well
  (see page 130)
350g hot-smoked trout fillets,
  at room temperature
4 eggs
juice of $\frac{1}{2}$ lemon, or to taste
small handful of chopped
  flat-leaf parsley leaves

BLOCK OF CREAMED COCONUT

Hardly the most exotic item in the storecupboard, blocks of creamed coconut have long been overtaken by the more widely used cans of coconut milk. But I find the blocks essential, more textured than the canned milk and certainly less wasteful, and use them constantly.

Southern coconut double bean curry

This is an everyday curry to which I turn often, as I always have cans of kidney beans in my larder as well as a block of creamed coconut and some tamarind paste. But it is certainly not everyday in taste. I add the green beans to make a complete meal, but you can leave them out, or add any other vegetable. The sugar subtly enhances the coconut flavour. Serve with rice.

Heat the oil in a medium-large non-stick saucepan. Add the mustard seeds and, once the popping subsides, add the onion and curry leaves and cook until the onion is soft and turning colour. Add the garlic and stir-fry for one minute, or until it smells cooked. Add the ground spices and some salt with a splash of water and cook for one or two minutes.

Add both types of beans and the coconut, with one-quarter of a bean can-full of water. Bring to the boil, then reduce the heat and simmer for five to seven minutes, or until everything comes together and has thickened slightly. Stir in the sugar and tamarind paste to taste, then adjust the seasoning to serve.

Serves 4

3 tbsp vegetable oil
¾ tsp mustard seeds
1 smallish red onion,
  finely chopped
10–12 fresh curry leaves
6 fat garlic cloves, grated
2 tsp ground coriander
½ tsp chilli powder, or to taste
½ tsp turmeric
1 tsp ground cumin
salt
2 x 400g cans kidney beans,
  drained and rinsed
75g green beans, topped, tailed
  and halved
60g creamed coconut block
  (around 7.5cm cube)
¾–1 tsp caster sugar, or
  to taste
2–3 tsp tamarind paste, or
  to taste

Hyderabadi sesame-coconut chicken korma

This is a great, easy korma recipe to have on hand: creamy, coconutty and mild. I have kept it white to reflect the flavours coming your way. This is based on a version from Hyderabad that uses a lot of different nuts and seeds. I have picked sesame in the form of tahini paste here, but, if you don't have tahini or don't like it, leave it out, it will still taste great, or add some pine nuts or peanuts instead. If you are an Indian food aficionado and have whole spices close to hand, add 2 black and 6 green cardamom pods, 3 cloves and a cinnamon stick and cut back on the prepared garam masala. I serve this korma sprinkled with store-bought crispy shallots that I keep at home, and eat it with Indian breads or a simple pilaf.

Blend together the ginger, yogurt, coconut, nuts, black pepper and some salt. (I use a hand-held blender for this.)

Heat the oil in a large non-stick saucepan, add the black cumin seeds and follow 30 seconds later with the onions; cook until soft and just browning at the edges. Add the garlic and cook for one minute, or until it smells cooked. Add the yogurt mix and cook, stirring, until it comes to the boil. Simmer, stirring very often, until it reduces completely and releases oil back into the pan, around 15 minutes.

Add the chicken, garam masala, tahini, a little more seasoning and about 200ml of water and bring to the boil. Reduce the heat and simmer until the chicken is cooked, five or six minutes: pierce a large piece to its centre, the juices should run clear. If there is any trace of pink, cook for a couple of minutes more, then test again. Take off the heat and stir in the cream and coriander. Taste, adjust the seasoning and serve, sprinkled with crispy shallots (if using).

time-saving star: *shop-bought crispy shallots*

Serves 4

40g root ginger, peeled weight, coarsely chopped
200g plain yogurt
70g creamed coconut block
40g ground almonds or cashews
½ tsp freshly ground black pepper
salt
4 tbsp vegetable oil
1 tsp black cumin seeds (optional, if you have them)
2 largish onions, finely sliced
4 fat garlic cloves, grated
8 skinless boneless chicken thighs, or 4 chicken breasts, cut into large cubes
2 tsp garam masala
1 tbsp tahini paste, or to taste
75–100ml single cream, to taste
small handful of chopped coriander leaves
handful of shop-bought crispy shallots, or see page 134 for home-made (optional)

Creamy coconut prawn curry

A special occasion curry inspired by the famous Bengali Chingri Malai speciality. It is essentially prawns, fresh coconut and a few rounding-out background flavours. This is my quick-and-easy version using canned coconut milk and creamed coconut to get that real coconut hit. If you are up for making your own, you need to extract one cup of thick coconut milk and one of thin from a good grated coconut. This is really lovely. I like to add a little lemon juice to balance the sweetness, but I leave it to you. The bigger and fresher the prawns the better, but even good-quality frozen prawns will do.

Heat the oil in a large non-stick saucepan. Add the whole spices and cook for 20–30 seconds. Add the chopped onion and cook until it has softened well, stirring occasionally.

Meanwhile, blend together the quartered onion, garlic and ginger until smooth, adding a little water if needed (I use my hand-held blender). Add to the cooked onion with salt and cook until any water used in blending has been absorbed and the onion has cooked and smells sweet. It will take at least 10 minutes.

Add the chilli powder and turmeric and give the pot a few good stirs. Add the coconut milk, bring to a gentle simmer and reduce the volume by one-third. Add the coconut cream and sugar and bring to the boil. You should have a lovely creamy curry sauce.

Throw in the prawns and simmer for three minutes, or until the prawns are cooked. Taste and balance the seasoning and sugar, adding a little squeeze of lemon juice if you like. It should be creamy but not cloying, so add a splash of just-boiled water from the kettle if you need to, then serve.

Serves 4

4 tbsp vegetable oil
2 Indian bay leaves
4 cloves
10cm cinnamon stick or
  shard of cassia bark
2 onions, one finely chopped,
  the other quartered
3 fat garlic cloves
15g root ginger, peeled weight,
  coarsely chopped
salt
¾ tsp chilli powder
1 tsp turmeric
2 x 400ml cans coconut milk
80–100g creamed coconut
  block
½–¾ tsp caster sugar, or
  to taste
500g raw tiger prawns, shelled
  weight, tails left on, deveined
squeeze of lemon juice
  (optional)

Roasted peanut fish curry

I once had an amazing fish in Hong Kong that was garnished with roasted peanuts and became a bit obsessed with the combination. I then read about a peanut and fish curry from Africa. It sparked my imagination and this is the result. It is sweet and sour and very delicious. For a different presentation, don't cube the fish, instead just season whole fillets on both sides, pat dry, fry in a non-stick pan, then plate up, spooning the curry around.

Heat the oil in a large non-stick saucepan and add the cumin seeds. Fry until sizzling and colouring. Add the onion and some salt and cook over a highish flame for three to four minutes, stirring once. Add the pepper to the onion and sauté for another few minutes or until the onions have coloured and the pepper is softening.

Meanwhile, blend together the tomatoes, ginger, garlic and the whole peanuts until smooth (I use a hand-held blender).

Add the ground spices to the onion mixture in the pan, give it a stir, then add the blended tomato mixture. Cook until completely reduced, about 15 minutes. It will be a thick paste and will release oil on the base of the pan.

Add the coconut and enough water to produce a thickish creamy sauce. Taste, adjust the seasoning and keep over a low heat. Add the fish and cook for four minutes, or until cooked through. Sprinkle over the crushed peanuts and serve.

Serves 4–5

4 tbsp vegetable oil
3 tsp cumin seeds
1 red onion, roughly chopped
salt
1 small red pepper, cut into 2.5cm cubes
4 ripe tomatoes, quartered
25g root ginger, peeled weight, coarsely chopped
6 fat garlic cloves
80g salted roasted peanuts, half lightly crushed
½ tsp chilli powder
1 tsp ground coriander
1½ tsp garam masala
450g creamed coconut block
4–5 firm white fish fillets, cut into large cubes

Sticky chicken livers on toast

This is great for a light supper, but also as a rustic starter for when you have friends around. It is warming, sweet and savoury and full of lovely contrasting textures.

Preheat the oven to 140°C/275°F/gas mark 1.

Lightly brush both sides of the slices of bread with a little olive oil and toast on both sides, either in a non-stick frying pan or a griddle pan, until lightly browned, around one or two minutes each side. Rub one side of each slice well with the piece of whole ginger to flavour the bread. Set aside in the oven to keep warm.

In a bowl, mix the livers with the seeds, garam masala, salt and black pepper, making sure they are all well coated.

Heat the 2 tbsp of olive oil in a frying pan with the butter. Once it is foaming, add the spiced chicken livers and sauté for five or six minutes, turning often. (Be careful, they tend to spit.) Add the grated ginger, dates and figs with the balsamic vinegar and stir well to coat everything. Cook for a further minute.

Remove the toasts from the oven and place on a serving plate or platter. Top each with a few Gem leaves and carefully spoon one-quarter of the livers on to each piece along with the dates and figs. Drizzle over the remaining sauce and serve.

Serves 4–5

4–5 slices of sourdough bread
2 tbsp olive oil, plus more to brush the bread
1 tsp finely grated root ginger, plus a peeled thumb-sized piece
400g chicken livers, cleaned
1 tsp nigella seeds
1 tsp lightly crushed fennel seeds
2 tsp garam masala
1 tsp salt
good pinch of freshly ground black pepper
30g butter
4 medjool dates, roughly slivered lengthways
2 fresh figs, quartered
2 tbsp balsamic vinegar
1 baby Gem lettuce, leaves washed but left whole

Black-spiced chicken and whole grain rasam

This spicy, hearty soup is based on a popular recipe from Chettinad, a region known for its black peppercorn dishes. The spices give the broth a dark colour but they are not as strong as they look. It is the ultimate comforting chicken soup, with the added benefit of having filling and nutty whole grains thrown in. I often buy a packet of mixed pre-cooked whole grains from the supermarket. If you only have raw farro or spelt, add in half the weight of the cooked grains used below at the same time as the chicken (check the cooking times on the packet though). As with all chicken soups, I use whole joints so they add their goodness to the dish.

Grind together all the whole spices for the spice blend to a fine powder.

Meanwhile, heat the oil in a large non-stick saucepan. Add the onions and curry leaves and cook until the onions are golden brown on the edges.

Add the garlic and ginger and cook gently for one minute before adding the spice blend with a good splash of water. Cook for another three or four minutes, then add the chicken thighs, stock and some salt. Pour in 500ml of water and bring to a boil. Reduce the heat to a simmer and cover the pan. Cook for 20 minutes or until the chicken is cooked, giving the pot an occasional stir. Pierce the largest chicken thigh; the juices that emerge should run clear with no trace of pink. If not, cover and cook for a few minutes longer, then check again.

Remove the chicken from the pan with a slotted spoon and add the grains to the soup, keeping it on a very gentle simmer. Once the chicken is cool enough to handle, tear the meat from the bones in large chunks and stir it back into the pot. Stir in the tamarind, taste and adjust the seasoning, then serve.

Serves 4

For the spice blend
1 star anise
1¾ tsp black peppercorns
3 tbsp coriander seeds
3 tsp cumin seeds
2 tsp fennel seeds
4 cloves
2.5cm shard of cassia bark or cinnamon stick

For the rasam
3–4 tbsp vegetable oil
2 onions, finely sliced
10 fresh curry leaves (optional)
5 fat garlic cloves, grated
25g root ginger, peeled weight, grated
5 large skinless bone-in chicken thighs
500ml chicken stock
salt
250g packet pre-cooked whole grains (I use a mix with spelt, wheat berries and brown rice)
¾ tsp tamarind paste, or to taste

time-saving star: *pre-cooked mixed grains*

Goan chicken cafreal

This recipe is so easy to make and doesn't even require any chopping! A vibrant herb sauce cooks alongside the chicken, each adding value to the other, until they are both cooked and the sauce is thick and clings to the meat. Serve with Indian bread.

As you begin your preparation, put the cashew nuts in a small bowl with enough water just to cover. Set aside to soak.

Slash each drumstick about three times at its thickest point.

For the green paste, grind all the whole spices to a powder. Whizz this together with the ginger, garlic, vinegar, coriander leaves and stalks, green chillies, salt and enough water to be able to blend until smooth, either in a hand-held blender or a mini food processor. Pour the resulting green paste over the chicken in a shallow dish, cover and leave to marinate for at least 20 minutes, or place in the fridge and leave for a couple of hours if you have time.

Heat the oil in a large non-stick pan. Add the chicken and marinade and bring to the boil, then reduce the heat, cover and simmer gently for 20–25 minutes, giving it the occasional stir. Blend together the cashew nuts and their soaking water with a hand-held blender and add to the sauce halfway through cooking time. The chicken is best cooked in its own juices, so try not to add too much water. Pierce the largest drumstick; the juices that emerge should run clear with no trace of pink. If not, cover and cook for a few minutes longer, then check again.

If there is too much liquid in the pan, uncover to cook it off for the last five minutes or so. The sauce should be thick enough to cling to the meat. Taste and adjust the seasoning to serve.

Serves 4–5

For the chicken
handful of cashew nuts
10 large skinless chicken
   drumsticks
4 tbsp vegetable oil

For the green paste
8 peppercorns
2 tsp coriander seeds
2.5cm cinnamon stick
6 cloves
6 green cardamom pods
1 rounded tsp cumin seeds
10g root ginger, peeled weight,
   coarsely chopped
8 largish garlic cloves
2$\frac{1}{2}$ tbsp red or white
   wine vinegar
240g coriander leaves and
   stalks, washed
2–4 green chillies, deseeded
salt

Super-quick Kashmiri kebabs with yogurt and dried apricots

These are absolutely delicious and the epitome of quick and easy Indian food. Kashmiri cuisine has many different lamb kebabs and meatballs. My version is a taste explosion of savoury, sweet, creamy, tangy, hot and cold. It is delicious and different. You can leave out the apricots if you prefer and scatter with shredded mint leaves. Serve with naan bread or rice.

Preheat the oven to 140°C/275°F/gas mark 1.

Put the lamb in a mixing bowl and add the breadcrumbs, ginger, garlic, salt, chilli, garam masala, 2 tsp of the ground fennel seeds, the pepper, coriander, mint and 4 tbsp of the yogurt. Mix well and divide into 16 balls, flattening each slightly.

I cook these in two large non-stick frying pans (if you don't have two pans, cook in two batches instead, keeping the first batch warm in the oven). Heat half the oil in each pan and add eight kebabs to each. Cook until golden on the base, then flip over and cook for another minute. Add 75ml of hot water, a good pinch of salt and half of the remaining ground fennel seeds to each pan; cover and cook for another three or four minutes.

Meanwhile, whisk the remaining yogurt with a little salt.

Once the kebabs are done, place on a warmed plate and cover with foil. Bubble up the liquid in the pans, scraping at any bits, until the juices reduce to 6–8 tbsp of stock. Pour this sauce over the kebabs. Top evenly with the yogurt and scatter over the apricots, with more mint if you like. Serve immediately.

Serves 4

- 400g minced lamb
- 6 tbsp breadcrumbs (around 2 small slices of bread)
- 15g root ginger, peeled weight, grated
- 4 fat garlic cloves, grated
- 3/4–1 tsp salt
- 1/2 tsp chilli powder, or to taste
- 1 1/2 tsp garam masala
- 3 1/2 tsp ground fennel seeds
- 1/3 tsp freshly ground black pepper
- 2 small handfuls of chopped coriander leaves
- 3 tbsp shredded mint leaves, plus more to serve (optional)
- 400g plain yogurt
- 3 tbsp vegetable oil
- 6 ready-to-eat dried apricots, cut into slivers

EASY ENTERTAINING

POT OF RICOTTA

I adore paneer, Indian fresh cheese, but the texture can vary and it isn't sold in all supermarkets. Mild, milky ricotta, available everywhere, makes an excellent substitute in baked recipes, such as those that follow. I always have a pot in the fridge.

Baked ricotta with chard

This lovely dish has been inspired by a vegetarian spinach and paneer kebab I tried years ago and loved. It has morphed in my kitchen into using ricotta instead of paneer, chard instead of spinach, and baked instead of fried! It makes a great vegetarian meal for friends. The chutney adds a lovely tangy, hot and garlicky contrast to the creamy dish and can be made in advance, even though it cooks itself at the same time as the ricotta.

Serves 5–6

softened butter, for the tin
2 tbsp olive oil
1½ tsp cumin seeds
1 largish onion, finely chopped
5 large garlic cloves,
  finely chopped
150g chard, coarsely shredded
½ tsp garam masala
salt and freshly ground
  black pepper
1 egg, lightly beaten
500g ricotta cheese
handful of pine nuts

Preheat the oven to 190°C/375°F/gas mark 5 and place a baking tray on the middle shelf. Butter well a 20cm round cake tin with a removable base.

Heat the olive oil in a large non-stick sauté pan. Add the cumin seeds and, once browned, add the onion and cook until golden on the edges. Add the garlic and cook for a minute or so. Stir in the chard, garam masala and some salt and cook for eight to 10 minutes, or until the chard has wilted. Remove from the heat.

Beat the egg into the ricotta until well blended, then stir in the vegetable mix. Taste and adjust the seasoning, adding ½ tsp of black pepper, or to taste. Pour the ricotta mixture into the tin, sprinkle over the pine nuts and place on the hot baking tray. Cook for 35 minutes, or until golden and set.

Quick-fire: Roasted red pepper, tomato and chilli chutney
Blend together 8 large garlic cloves, 1 red chilli, deseeded, and 6 ripe vine tomatoes, quartered, until smooth (I use my hand-held blender). Heat 2 tbsp of vegetable oil in a saucepan and add the blended ingredients with some salt. Cook, stirring occasionally, until the mixture has reduced and begins to release oil into the pan, around 25 minutes. Taste; it should taste harmonious. Stir in 1 roast, skinned pepper from a jar, chopped, and cook for another few minutes to warm through. Serves 6.

Ricotta-stuffed aubergines in tomato sauce

This dish is so absolutely delicious that once you make it, you feel like doing it again the following night. The combination of the meaty aubergines with the creamy ricotta is a real taste sensation. I often add in a couple of handfuls of spinach for some healthy greens. In the summer, use fresh tomatoes; in the winter, use a can. I serve this dish with salad and naan or crusty bread on the side.

Blend the tomatoes with a little water until smooth (I use a hand-held blender). Lightly season the aubergines.

Heat the oil in a large non-stick saucepan. Add the fennel seeds and cook for 10 seconds, then tip in the onion and cook until lightly browned on the edges. Add the garlic and cook for a minute or so. Add the blended tomatoes, tomato purée, chilli, coriander and seasoning. Cook over a moderate heat, stirring occasionally, until it thickens into a paste and releases oil, around 15 minutes. Taste, it should taste harmonious. Pour in 150ml of water, bring to the boil and simmer gently for four to five minutes, or until it all comes together into a creamy sauce. Taste and adjust the seasoning, adding a pinch of sugar if the tomatoes are too acidic.

Meanwhile, cook the aubergines: heat a good drizzle of oil in a large frying pan and add as many slices of aubergines as will fit in the pan; cook over a medium heat until golden brown on the underside, then turn over and repeat, it takes around three minutes a side. Remove and place on a plate. Repeat with the remaining slices until they are all cooked. (You can also cook these in an oven preheated to 180°C/350°F/gas mark 4; brush liberally with oil, season and place on a baking tray, then cook for 15–20 minutes, or until completely soft.)

Mix together the ricotta, red onion and mint and season. Place 1 tbsp of this on to each slice of aubergine, about 2.5cm from the edge. Carefully roll them up into fat short logs, patting in any escaping ricotta. Place the rolls seam-side down in the tomato sauce, spoon over some of the sauce and gently heat through for three or four minutes. Serve hot.

Serves 3–4

3 tomatoes, quartered and deseeded
salt and freshly ground black pepper
2 aubergines, cut into 1cm slices lengthways (you need about 12 slices in all)
3 tbsp vegetable oil, plus more for the aubergines
¾ tsp fennel seeds
1 largish onion, chopped
4 fat garlic cloves, grated
2 tsp tomato purée
½ fat red chilli, finely sliced
1 tsp ground coriander
caster sugar, if needed
225g ricotta cheese
½ small red onion, finely chopped
1 tbsp shredded mint leaves

Oven-baked fish with herb dressing and lemon-bean mash

A really summery recipe, perfect for easy entertaining... or just to make because you feel like it. Sea bream is a lovely fish that works very well here, but feel free to experiment with others. The coriander chutney is really quick to do (I whizz up a batch and keep it in the freezer) and the bean mash adds a lovely earthy creaminess. This is great with one of the many salads in this book, or with a pilaf and Carom Seed Sautéed Spinach (see page 135).

Preheat the oven to 190°C/375°F/gas mark 5. For the fish, mix together the lemon juice, olive oil and garlic and season.

Boil the potatoes for the mash until tender, then drain and mash them.

Meanwhile, score one side of each fish three times. Season the fish on both sides and in the cavity.

Using 1 tbsp of the chutney for each fish, rub half into the slashes on the upper surface and place the rest in the cavity. Place on a non-stick baking tray, slashed-side up, with the lemon slices tucked underneath. Repeat to coat all the fish. Drizzle about 1 tbsp of the lemon juice mixture over each fish. Place in the oven and cook for 18–20 minutes or until done.

Meanwhile, heat the olive oil for the mash and add the panch phoran; once the popping subsides, add the spring onion and sauté for one minute or until slightly soft. Take off the heat.

Blend the beans with the crème fraîche and milk (I use a hand-held blender) and season well with salt and pepper. Pour and scrape into the pan with the potato mash. Warm through, giving the pot a good stir. Taste, adjust the seasoning and add lemon juice to taste, it should be nice and tangy.

To serve, mix the remaining lemon juice mixture into the remaining chutney. Remove the fish from the oven, baste with the tray juices and place on warmed plates with the chutney mixture and lemon mash.

Serves 4

For the fish and dressing
4 tbsp lemon juice, plus a few lemon slices
4 tbsp olive oil
4 garlic cloves, grated
salt and freshly ground black pepper
4 medium sea bream, scaled, trimmed and cleaned
8 tbsp Tangy Coriander Chutney (see page 154)

For the cannellini bean mash
250g floury potatoes (such as Maris Piper or King Edwards)
2 tbsp extra virgin olive oil
$\frac{1}{2}$ tsp panch phoran (or see page 122 to make your own)
1 large spring onion, sliced on the diagonal
115g ($\frac{1}{2}$ a can) cannellini beans, drained weight, rinsed
4 tbsp crème fraîche
3 tbsp milk
2 tbsp lemon juice, or to taste

Burmese chicken and coconut curry

I have never been to Burma, but this particular dish has well and truly made it to India and has become dinner party fare. I love it. It is impressive, but requires little more than making a curry and buying accompaniments.

Heat the oil in a large non-stick saucepan. Add the onions and cook until golden brown on the edges. Meanwhile, blend together the ginger and garlic with a small splash of water to help it become smooth (I use a hand-held blender). Add to the onions and cook until the water has dried off and the garlic has had a minute to cook; add a little water if it starts to stick. Spoon in the gram flour and stir for a minute before adding a good splash of water and the powdered spices. Cook for three or four minutes.

Add the chicken stock and coconut milk, bring to the boil, then reduce the heat and simmer for five minutes. Add the chicken, tomato and creamed coconut and return to the boil, then reduce the heat and cook gently for another seven or eight minutes, or until cooked through. Stir in the lemon juice, taste and adjust the salt and lemon juice to taste.

Meanwhile, prepare as many of the accompaniments as you like, or can be bothered to make, and offer them at the table in small bowls and dishes. These are what make this dish memorable, so the more the merrier!

Serves 4, can be doubled

2 tbsp vegetable oil
2 onions, sliced
30g root ginger, peeled weight, coarsely chopped
7 large garlic cloves
2 rounded tbsp gram (chickpea) flour
¾ tsp turmeric
1 tbsp ground coriander
2 tsp ground cumin
2 tsp garam masala
250ml chicken stock
400ml can coconut milk
500g skinless boneless chicken thighs, each cut into 3 chunks
1 large tomato, finely chopped
60g creamed coconut
2 tbsp lemon juice, or to taste
salt

For the accompaniments
shop-bought crispy fried shallots, or see page 134 for home-made
2 spring onions, sliced
3 hard-boiled eggs, quartered
2 long red chillies, finely sliced
handful of roasted peanuts
egg noodles (around 2 x 400g packets), cooked according to the packet instructions
handful of chopped coriander leaves
lime wedges

time-saving star: *shop-bought crispy shallots*

Tamarind chicken curry

This is a fabulous curry inspired by South Indian ingredients. The tamarind adds a fruity sourness. Using chicken joints is quite important here, as you need the flavour from the bones to round off and balance the tamarind; it might take 20 minutes longer than boneless meat, but the curry almost cooks itself and is worth it. Tamarind brands vary in strength and viscosity, so you will need to add to taste. Serve with Indian breads; paratha would be my first choice.

Heat the oil in a non-stick saucepan. Add the mustard seeds and, once the popping dies down, add the curry leaves and follow with the onions; cook until well browned. Meanwhile, blend the ginger and garlic with a little water until smooth (I use a hand-held blender) and add to the cooked onions. Cook off the excess water, then fry the paste for one minute. Add the ground spices and some salt with a small splash of water and cook for a minute.

Add the chicken and chillies and stir well in the masala. Pour in enough water to come halfway up the chicken. Bring to a boil, then cover, reduce the heat and simmer gently until nearly cooked through, around 30 minutes, stirring occasionally and adding a splash more water if necessary.

Uncover and cook off any excess liquid; the sauce should be about the consistency of double cream. As you do this, incorporate the tamarind and continue cooking until you have a consistency you like. Taste, adjust the seasoning and serve.

Serves 4–6

5 tbsp vegetable oil
1 tsp mustard seeds
15 fresh curry leaves
3 onions, sliced
30g root ginger, peeled weight, coarsely chopped
10 fat garlic cloves
1 rounded tbsp ground coriander
$\frac{2}{3}$ tsp turmeric
1 tsp ground cumin
1$\frac{1}{2}$ tsp garam masala
$\frac{1}{4}$ tsp freshly ground black pepper
salt
8 big skinless bone-in chicken thighs or 800g other chicken joints
2–5 green chillies, whole but pierced with the tip of a knife (optional)
1$\frac{1}{2}$–2 tsp tamarind paste (see recipe introduction), dissolved in 4 tbsp of hot water

SLOW
EASY
COOK

Duck and prune curry

This is a special occasion dish that marries North Indian flavours with duck and juicy French Agen prunes for a lovely, complex flavour that is worthy of anyone's entertaining repertoire. Serve with simple pilaf rice or even some creamy mashed potatoes. If you are not confident about skinning the duck legs, ask your butcher to do it for you.

Blend the tomatoes, ginger, garlic and spices until smooth (I use a hand-held blender for this).

Heat the oil in a wide non-stick saucepan, add the onions and sauté until they have browned well. Stir in the duck, blended tomato mixture and some salt. Bring to the boil. Cover, reduce the heat to a gentle simmer and cook the duck until it is very tender, 60–80 minutes. Give the legs an occasional turn in the pan as you stir the sauce; the more you stir, the more homogenous it becomes. Add a splash of water from the kettle only when necessary; the cooking liquid should never come more than halfway up the duck.

When the duck is done, add the prunes and half the coriander, then adjust the consistency of the sauce by either boiling off excess water or – more likely – adding a small splash from the kettle; it should be creamy and delicious. Taste and adjust the seasoning. Serve sprinkled with the remaining coriander and swirl over a little cream or sour cream, if using.

Serves 4

2 tomatoes, quartered
30g ginger, peeled weight, coarsely chopped
6 fat garlic cloves
1 rounded tsp ground cumin
½–¾ tsp chilli powder, or paprika if you prefer colour without heat
2 tsp ground coriander
2 tsp garam masala
4–5 tbsp vegetable oil
2 onions, finely chopped
4 duck legs (drumsticks and thighs together), skinned
salt and freshly ground black pepper
large handful of ready-to-eat Agen prunes
handful of coriander leaves
swirl of cream or sour cream (optional)

Goan-style roast pork belly

A delicious combination of flavours. I was taught this recipe by a Goan, Russ D'Costa, who pot-roasted his pork belly. He had mentioned making a caramel somewhere in the middle and adding it to the pan... which he then forgot as we chatted. I was imagining the sticky sweet, spiced results and waited patiently until the very end when he admitted his mistake. However, the pork was so fantastic, spicy, tangy and flavourful that I don't see how the sweetness would have added anything. My version is roasted in the oven for ease and for the lovely crackling. Serve it with mash, or Goan Tomato Rice or Goan Coconut Rice (see pages 80 and 130), or just with a simple salad such as Lightly Spiced Salad of Celeriac with Capers (see page 138).

The night before cooking – or at least the morning before a supper – score the skin of your belly of pork with a sharp knife at 1cm intervals, or ask your butcher to do so. Place it on a trivet in the sink, skin-side up, and pour a kettle of boiling water over the top (this helps to make the crackling crisp up). Pat dry with kitchen paper.

Place the pork on a board, skin-side down and, using a fork, pierce the meat aggressively all over the flesh and sides – but not the skin – to help the marinade to penetrate. I pierce around 40–50 times in all.

Blend together all the ingredients for the marinade with 2 tbsp of water until smooth (I use a hand-held blender), then rub it all over the flesh, leaving the skin free of marinade.

Place the pork, skin-side up, in a roasting tray in which it fits snugly. Place in the fridge (unwrapped so that the skin can dry out) overnight, or for at least a good five to six hours, making sure all the marinade is on the underside.

When you're ready to cook, return the meat to room temperature and preheat the oven to 150°C/300°F/gas mark 2. Mix together the ¾ tsp of salt and the ground fennel seeds, sprinkle evenly over the skin and rub in well. Pour 240ml of water into the tray with the pork (it should not come up to the skin) and place it in the centre of the oven. Cook for two and a half hours. Increase the oven temperature to 220°C/425°F/gas mark 7 and cook for a final 30 minutes, checking the water every 10 minutes and adding a splash more if it dries up.

Remove the pork from the oven and allow it to rest for 15–20 minutes, covered in foil. Spoon off any excess fat from the tray, then taste and adjust the seasoning of the juices, adding the maple syrup if you like, and reducing them over a medium heat if they seem too thin. Serve the pork with the remaining pan juices; there won't be a lot but what remains will be intense.

Serves 6

For the pork
1.2kg belly of pork
¾ tsp salt
1½ tsp fennel seeds, lightly roasted, then ground (see page 92)
1 tbsp maple syrup (optional)

For the marinade
1 tsp freshly ground black pepper
4 fat garlic cloves
15g root ginger, peeled weight, coarsely chopped
1 tsp chilli powder
¾ tsp ground cumin
⅓ tsp turmeric
1 scant tsp salt
1 tsp red or white wine vinegar
juice of ½ lemon

SLOW EASY COOK

Pickle-flavoured lamb curry

A lovely, full-bodied, North Indian-style lamb that is really easy to make and truly rewarding to eat. Panch phoran is a mix of five seeds that you can buy in Indian markets, virtual or real, and consists of cumin, nigella, fennel, fenugreek and mustard seeds. It adds a great, distinctive note, but you can also make your own (see below). Serve this curry with Indian breads.

Heat the oil in a large saucepan. (If you are using mustard oil, bring it to smoking point and then cool for 30 seconds before continuing.) Add the panch phoran, reduce the heat and cook until the popping dies down. Add the onions and cook over a high heat until they have browned nicely on the edges.

Meanwhile, blend together the ginger and garlic with a good splash of water until smooth (I use my hand-held blender). Add to the onions with some salt and the cumin, coriander and chilli powder. Cook for about two minutes or until the water has evaporated and the garlic has had a chance to fry.

Add the lamb and brown over a highish flame until coloured all over, tossing often so the spices don't burn. Add a splash of water to deglaze the pan, then add the tomatoes and chillies. Bring to the boil, cover, reduce the heat and cook until the lamb is tender, around 1¼ hours. Stir occasionally to make sure nothing is sticking. You shouldn't need water, but pour in a splash if you are worried it might burn.

Stir in the garam masala and coriander leaves. Taste, adjust the seasoning and serve.

Serves 4

6 tbsp mustard or vegetable oil
2 rounded tsp panch phoran
2 largish onions, chopped
25g root ginger, peeled weight, coarsely chopped
9 fat garlic cloves
salt and freshly ground black pepper
1 tsp ground cumin
2 tsp ground coriander
½–¾ tsp chilli powder
600g boneless leg of lamb, cut into 2.5cm cubes
4 tomatoes, cut into wedges
2–4 green chillies (optional), pierced with the tip of a knife
1½ tsp garam masala
good handful of chopped coriander leaves

make it better: *mix your own panch phoran*

If you don't have panch phoran, you can make up your own mixture combining the five different kinds of seeds used: cumin, nigella, fennel, mustard and fenugreek. Add as many of the different seeds as you have in equal amounts, but using just half the amount of fenugreek as of the others. Mix your panch phoran in small amounts and measure out only what is needed in a recipe.

Beef rendang

This is sweet, rich, spiced and lightly coconutty, but the star is the meltingly soft beef. This slightly Indianised version of the South-east Asian classic is easy and needs little more than 20 minutes of your attention. It works really well; in fact so well that I promise you will crave this dish. Serve it with rice.

Preheat the oven to 180°C/350°F/gas mark 4.

To make the spice paste, blend together the shallots, garlic, ginger, chillies and lemon grass, adding a little water to help. (I use my hand-held blender.)

Heat the oil in a medium-large ovenproof saucepan. Add the whole spices and follow with the spice paste, cooking until all the excess liquid has dried up. Stir-fry the paste for five to seven minutes. If it threatens to burn, add a splash of water.

Add the beef and onions and cook for another three to five minutes in the paste, stirring often, or until all the beef has some colour. Add the coconut milk, lime zest, palm sugar and the whole bruised lemon grass stalks. Bring to a boil, then cover the pan and transfer to the oven. Cook for 1½ hours, or until the beef is meltingly soft. Check halfway through, stirring in any browned bits on the edges.

When done, replace the pot on the hob and stir in the tamarind paste, creamed coconut and garam masala. Taste and adjust the seasoning, also adding the lime juice to taste. Serve hot.

Serves 6

For the spice paste
6 shallots, peeled and
 quartered
8 fat garlic cloves, peeled
30g root ginger, peeled weight,
 roughly chopped
3–4 large red chillies, halved,
 deseeded if you prefer
2 lemon grass stalks, trimmed
 and chopped

For the rendang
5 tbsp vegetable oil
6 green cardamom pods
2 star anise
2 shards of cassia bark or
 cinnamon sticks
1kg good chuck stewing beef,
 cut into 2.5cm cubes
2 onions, sliced
400g can of coconut milk
finely grated zest and juice of
 1 lime
2 tsp palm sugar or other sugar
2 lemon grass stalks, bruised
1½ tsp tamarind paste,
 or to taste
50g creamed coconut, dissolved
 in 50ml hot water
1 tsp garam masala
salt and freshly ground
 black pepper

Spiced roast leg of lamb

For Indians, roasting a leg of lamb is reserved for special occasions. The lamb is normally marinated overnight for the spices to have time to penetrate deep into the flesh, then roasted slowly for hours until the meat falls off the bone. This is an easier version of that special dish and, while it needs lots of spices, it cooks itself in the oven, so is a really easy entertaining option. You can serve this with an elegant pilaf, naan, vegetables or salads, or just a lovely raita, depending on how you like to eat. The longer you marinate this lamb, the better the result; overnight is best.

Using a spice grinder or a mortar and pestle, grind all the whole spices and bay leaves to a fine powder.

Blend together the ginger, garlic, vinegar, oil and as much of the yogurt as you need to make a smooth paste (I use a hand-held blender). Add the ground spices, chilli powder, salt and remaining yogurt.

Weigh the lamb and make a note of its weight. Place the meat in a large shallow dish and make lots of slits all over the surface with a small sharp knife. Spread over the marinade, massaging well to make sure it goes into the slits and the lamb is well and evenly covered. Cover and leave to marinate in the fridge for as long as possible, ideally overnight, but for a minimum of two to three hours.

When you're ready to cook, return the lamb to room temperature and preheat the oven to 180°C/350°F/gas mark 4. Place the lamb in a baking tray along with every last bit of marinade. Cover with a lid, or with some foil, and slide on to the middle shelf of the oven. Now cook for 22 minutes per 500g of weight, adding 20 minutes extra at the end. After the meat has been roasting for one hour, uncover the dish and pour 100ml of water into the tray. Baste every 20–30 minutes, keeping an eye on the moisture levels and adding a splash more water if the tray dries out.

Once done, take the meat out of the oven, cover with foil and a tea towel and rest for 15–20 minutes before carving. Skim any excess fat from the pan juices, taste them for seasoning, then serve them with the lamb.

Serves 6–8

9 cloves
8 green cardamom pods
3 black cardamom pods
½–¾ tsp black peppercorns
7.5cm cinnamon stick
1½ tsp cumin seeds
3 dried bay leaves
75g root ginger, peeled weight, coarsely chopped
35g garlic cloves
3 tsp red wine vinegar
2 tbsp vegetable oil
150g plain yogurt
¾ tsp chilli powder
1¾ tsp salt
1.8–2kg leg of lamb (I like mine half-boned by the butcher)

SLOW
EASY
COOK

Rajasthani-spiced venison curry

Quick to cook, this is meant to be a spicy dish, and can also be made with lamb. If you want to make it when you have time to spare, buy a cut of stewing venison and cook for longer until tender for a fuller flavour. Serve with a raita and Indian breads.

Soak the chillies (if using) for 30 minutes in hot water, then drain.

Heat the oil in a non-stick pan and sear the meat on all sides. Place in a bowl. Cook the onion over a medium-high heat until golden brown on the edges.

Blend the ginger, garlic and dried chillies, if using, with water until smooth. Add to the pan and cook until the garlic smells cooked.

Add the yogurt and ground spices (including the chilli powder, if you didn't use dried chillies) and stir until it comes to a boil; the masala will reduce to a thick paste and release oil into the pan. At this point, add a little water. Return the venison with its juices, season and coat in the masala. Add the stock. Bring to a boil while stirring, then reduce the heat and simmer gently for four or five minutes for a slightly pink interior. Taste and adjust the seasoning, adding lemon juice, if you like. Add the coriander and serve sprinkled with crispy shallots, if using.

Serves 4

3–4 dried chillies, ideally Kashmiri, or ½–1 tsp chilli powder
4 tbsp vegetable oil, or ghee, or a mixture
500g venison steak, cut into 2.5cm cubes
1 onion, sliced
30g root ginger, peeled weight, grated
6 fat garlic cloves
150ml plain yogurt
¼ tsp ground cloves, or 6 whole cloves
3 tsp ground coriander
½ tsp ground cumin
1 tsp garam masala
salt and freshly ground black pepper
200ml chicken stock
lemon juice, to taste (optional)
large handful of chopped coriander leaves
shop-bought crispy fried shallots, or see page 134 for home-made (optional)

time-saving star: shop-bought crispy shallots

Spiced aubergines with cannellini beans

This is a finger-licking tasty, balanced vegetarian curry. I like to add a little cream as I think it brings all the flavours together, but it is not essential and creaminess can come from some raita served on the side. If you have a good pure mustard oil, that will add a lot of flavour, but it first needs to be heated until it smokes and then cooled a little before continuing. Serve with Indian breads and raita, and maybe some greens.

Heat the oil in a large non-stick sauté pan. Add 2 tsp of the panch phoran and cook until the popping starts to die down. Add the onion and ginger and cook until soft and browning on the edges.

Meanwhile, prepare the aubergines by trimming the stalks and halving them lengthways and, if necessary, crossways if they are long.

Add the garlic to the pan and cook for one minute or until beginning to colour. Stir in the tomatoes, spices and some salt with a small splash of water. Bring to a simmer, then reduce the heat, cover and simmer gently for 10–15 minutes or until the tomatoes have really broken down.

Add the aubergines, cover and continue to cook very gently for another 15 minutes or until they are soft, stirring occasionally; try not to add any more water as this dish tastes best when cooked in its own juices.

Meanwhile, toast the remaining 1 tsp of panch phoran in a dry pan, shaking, until the seeds start to darken. Pour straight into a mortar and grind to a fine powder.

Stir the beans and the roasted ground panch phoran into the pan, taste and adjust the seasoning, adding the sugar if the tomatoes are too tart. Cook for another couple of minutes, stir in the coriander and serve with a little cream, if using.

Serves 4

4 tbsp vegetable or mustard oil
3 tsp panch phoran (see page 122 to make your own)
1 onion, chopped
20g root ginger, peeled weight, sliced into julienne
450g long Japanese aubergines, washed well
4 garlic cloves, grated
3 largish ripe vine tomatoes, cut into smallish wedges
$\frac{1}{2}$ tsp turmeric
2 tsp ground coriander
1 rounded tsp roasted ground cumin (see page 92)
1 rounded tsp garam masala
$\frac{1}{4}$–$\frac{1}{2}$ tsp chilli powder, or to taste
salt
400g can cannellini beans, drained and rinsed
a pinch of caster sugar (optional)
large handful of chopped coriander leaves
good drizzle of single cream (optional)

QUICK SIDES

PACK OF BASMATI

Goan coconut rice

This lovely, rich-flavoured dish goes with everything: lamb, chicken, fish, vegetables or lentils. I prefer it with less coconut, but lots of people prefer the stickier version with more; I have given both options, just adjust the quantities of coconut milk and water. Any leftovers make delicious coconut rice cakes (press into flat balls and fry gently on both sides in a little oil).

Once the rice has been washed, leave it to soak in fresh water while you start the cooking. Heat the oil in a non-stick saucepan. Add the whole spices, cook for 30–40 seconds, then add the onion. Sauté until soft and caramelising on the edges. Drain the rice and add to the onion, stirring until all the grains are coated in the oil and any excess water has dried off.

Add the coconut milk and water, in the ratio you prefer, to give a total liquid volume of 760ml. Season with salt to taste (see overleaf). Bring to a boil, cover and reduce the heat to its lowest setting. Cook until the rice is cooked through, around 10 minutes. You will need to stir the pan a few times to make sure it does not stick.

Increase the flame, uncover and cook off any excess liquid for one or two minutes. Turn the flame off, cover and allow the rice to steam for five minutes. Serve with one or both of the toppings, if you like.

Serves 4

300g basmati rice, well washed (see below)
2 tbsp vegetable oil
1 cinnamon stick
1 tsp black peppercorns
6 cloves
1 red onion, finely sliced
360–400ml coconut milk
360–400ml water
salt

Optional toppings
handful of roasted cashew nuts or peanuts
shop-bought crispy fried shallots, or see page 134 for home-made

Perfect, foolproof boiled rice

The technique to achieve perfect, fluffy rice is actually really easy. This is how we have always made it in my family.

Wash the rice well in several changes of water: I place it in a saucepan and pour over water. Swirl well with your fingers to dislodge the starch on the grains and pour off. Repeat until the water runs clear. Cover with at least 7.5cm of fresh water.

Bring to a boil and bubble (as you would pasta) for seven to eight minutes. Try a grain, it should be ready; if not cook for another minute and check again. Drain, then return the rice to the pan and the heat to dry off excess water for one minute. Turn off the heat, cover and allow to steam for eight to 10 minutes.

70–80g good-quality basmati rice per person

Dill and spinach pilaf

Adding herbs to rice is such a quick and easy way of giving flavour to delicate rice dishes. The rice and dill combination was popular with the Armenian immigrants who settled in India many centuries ago. This lovely pilaf can be eaten as it is with yogurt, or served alongside lots of the other dishes in this book, from a lentil curry to roasted or grilled meats. If you have the spices at home, add a cinnamon stick and a few cloves with the cumin.

Once the rice has been washed, leave it to soak in fresh water while you start the cooking. Heat the oil in a non-stick saucepan. Add the cumin seeds and, once they have browned, add the onions and some salt, cooking until the onions are golden on the edges. Add the garlic and stir until cooked, around one minute.

Add the spinach and dill and stir until the spinach has wilted. Drain the rice, add it to the pan and give it a few good turns to amalgamate with the other ingredients. Add the stock or water and taste and season the liquid (see below), adding pepper at this stage as well as salt. Bring to a boil and boil for a few minutes, then reduce the heat right down, cover and cook the rice until done, around eight minutes. Check to see if the grains are soft, then turn the heat off, stir in a little lemon juice with a fork, replace the lid and leave to steam for five minutes.

Serves 4

300g basmati rice, well washed
  (see page 130)
3 tbsp vegetable oil
2 tsp cumin seeds
2 smallish red onions,
  thinly sliced
salt and freshly ground
  black pepper
3 fat garlic cloves, chopped
225g baby spinach, washed
100g dill fronds, chopped
600ml vegetable or chicken
  stock, or water
lemon juice, to taste

make it better: *well-seasoned rice*

Plain boiled rice should be just that: plain. However, if the rice is part of an assemblage of vegetables, or to serve as the basis for a meal, such as in a biryani, you must check the seasoning of the water before cooking the rice. Pour in the measured cooking water, then taste the water: rice needs lots of seasoning so, if anything, it should taste slightly overseasoned to your palate. Adjust the seasoning of the liquid until it is correct to your taste.

Elegant pistachio and dried fig pilaf

A sophisticated pilaf to serve to friends, lovely with any curry, and also brilliant with some of the roasted meats in this book, perhaps with a creamy raita on the side. The pistachios add a lovely fragrant nuttiness and the dried fruit a sweet chewiness that works well with the spiced rice. You can vary the dried fruits as you like.

Once the rice has been washed, leave it to soak in fresh water while you cook. Heat 1cm of oil in a large non-stick saucepan. Add the onion and fry for five to seven minutes, or until deep golden but not brown (it will continue cooking once you take it out). Using a slotted spoon, remove the onion and place on kitchen paper to crisp up. Remove most of the oil from the pan, leaving 3 tbsp.

Reheat the 3 tbsp of oil, add all the spices except the saffron and cook for 40 seconds or so. Add the pistachios, figs, drained rice and saffron. Give the pot a few good stirs and add 400ml of water. Taste the water and add seasoning to taste (see page 133).

Bring to the boil, then cover and reduce the heat to its lowest. Cook undisturbed for seven to eight minutes. Check a grain and, if the rice is done, turn off the heat, cover and leave to steam for a further five to seven minutes. To serve, pile into a bowl or platter and garnish with the onions.

Serves 3

200g basmati rice, well washed (see page 130)
vegetable oil
1 large onion, finely sliced
1 tsp cumin seeds
7.5cm shard of cassia bark or cinnamon stick
3 cloves
1 bay leaf
4 green cardamom pods
40–50g pistachios
3 large ready-to-eat dried figs, chopped, or 2 tbsp sultanas
good pinch of saffron
salt and freshly ground black pepper

Roasted spiced cauliflower

This is a very easy dish that basically cooks itself. The flavours are simple and work really well with this much-overlooked vegetable. Please do add the cauliflower leaves as instructed; they become beautifully crispy and, in our family, we fight over who gets them!

Preaheat the oven to 180°C/350°F/gas mark 4.

Mix all the spices and ginger together in a bowl with the salt and toss in the florets and the leaves. Place everything in a non-stick baking tray and drizzle over the oil. Toss again and place on the middle shelf of the oven.

Roast for 20–25 minutes, or until done to your liking, then serve immediately.

Serves 4

1 tsp garam masala
1 tsp cumin seeds
½ tsp turmeric
½ tsp nigella seeds
15g root ginger, peeled weight, finely shredded
½ tsp salt
1 cauliflower, cut into florets, keeping the outer leaves
4 tbsp olive oil

Carom seed sautéed spinach

This is a really simple but flavourful dish that goes with everything. I like to use whole leaf spinach as I prefer the texture, but you can use baby spinach. Carom seeds have a flavour reminiscent of thyme; if you don't have them, add a few sprigs of thyme with the garlic instead.

Heat the oil in a sauté pan on a gentle flame and add the garlic and carom seeds; cook gently for one minute. Add the cumin, give it a stir and follow with the spinach and salt. Cook until the leaves have wilted and the water has dried up.

Add the butter and lemon juice to taste, adjust the seasoning and serve.

Serves 3–4

1 tbsp vegetable oil
4 large garlic cloves, chopped
⅓ tsp carom seeds
1 tsp ground cumin
500g whole leaf or baby spinach, tough stalks removed, washed well
salt
big knob of unsalted butter
small squeeze of lemon juice

Quickest ever tarka dal

This is the fastest recipe for this famous dish I have ever written, but it is just as tasty as any other. Red lentils cook very quickly, are easy to digest and lovely and creamy, so they're a perfect choice. I normally make the tarka as the lentils cook, it does mean washing two pans but it saves a lot of time. This is delicious with Indian breads, rice and... well, everything!

Bring the lentils to a boil in a saucepan. Once the scum rises to the top, skim it off and add the turmeric. Leave to simmer while you make the tarka.

For the tarka, heat the oil and butter in a frying pan and add the cumin seeds. Once they darken, add the onion and cook until soft and colouring on the edges. Add the garlic and cook gently for one minute, then add the tomatoes, spices and some salt and cook until the tomatoes soften and the whole thing reduces into a paste and releases oil back into the pan, around 15 minutes.

Add the masala to the lentils, making sure you get all of it out of the pan. Cook the lentils for another six to eight minutes or so, or until the whole thing comes together and looks homogenous. It should neither be too thick nor too watery.

Taste and adjust the seasoning, adding a good squeeze of lemon juice. Serve in warmed bowls, topped with a swirl of yogurt and some crispy onions, if you like, and the coriander.

Serves 4

For the dal
100g red lentils (*masoor dal*)
½ tsp turmeric
juice of ½ lemon
plain yogurt, to serve (optional)
shop-bought crispy fried onions, or see page 134 for home-made (optional)
small handful of chopped coriander leaves

For the tarka
1 tbsp vegetable oil
2 tbsp butter
¾ tsp cumin seeds
1 very small onion, chopped
4 fat garlic cloves, grated
2 smallish tomatoes, chopped
2 tsp ground coriander
¼–½ tsp chilli powder
salt

time-
saving star:
*shop-bought
crispy
onions*

Roasted carrots with dates

A really lovely sweet, spicy side dish. The roasting intensifies and marries all the flavours with the dates, adding a sweet, chewy element. Try and use medjool dates, as the dried dates you get in packets often lack the caramel flavours of 'proper' dates. Look for ginger that is heavy for its size, as it will contain the most juice. To make the ginger juice needed here, grate root ginger, place it in a nylon sieve over a bowl and press on it. The juice comes through.

Preheat the oven to 220°C/425°F/gas mark 7.

Toss the carrots with the oil, seasoning, ground spices and ginger juice and place on a baking sheet in the middle of the oven. Roast for 20–22 minutes or until done. Stir in the dates and serve.

Serves 4

6 carrots, peeled and cut into
  5cm batons
2–3 tbsp olive oil
sea salt and freshly ground
  black pepper
1½ tsp garam masala
⅓ tsp ground cinnamon
⅓ tsp chilli powder
1½ tsp ginger juice (see recipe
  introduction)
3–4 mejdool dates, depending
  on how big they are (those
  I buy are huge), chopped

Lightly spiced salad of celeriac with capers

I have always loved celeriac, especially in a rémoulade; it adds creaminess and a faint anise flavour to anything it is paired with. Here is my updated and slightly Indianised version of that simple dish. It goes with so many dishes in this book, especially with fish and grilled meats.

Add the juice of ½ the lemon to a large saucepan of cold water. Thinly slice or shave the celeriac and drop it into the water, to prevent discolouration. Bring the saucepan to the boil and cook for two minutes, then drain the celeriac and tip immediately into a bowl of cold water. Give the saucepan a wipe.

Meanwhile, mix the mayonnaise, yogurt, 4 tsp more lemon juice, the mustard, capers and a good pinch of salt and black pepper in a bowl. Heat the olive oil in a pan, tilting it so that the oil collects at the bottom. Add the panch phoran and, once the sizzling starts to die down, pour it into the bowl.

Drain the celeriac once more, lightly press down on the slices or shavings to extract all the excess water, then add to the mayonnaise bowl with the coriander leaves, stirring well to mix. Taste and adjust the seasoning to serve.

Serves 4

juice of 1 lemon
500g celeriac, peeled weight
4 tbsp mayonnaise
2 tbsp Greek yogurt
2 tsp Dijon mustard
2 tbsp capers, drained
  and rinsed
salt and freshly ground
  black pepper
1 tsp extra virgin olive oil
1 tsp panch phoran
handful of chopped
  coriander leaves

Spiced sautéed potatoes with dill

Indians will always have a favourite spiced potato dish in their repertoire. I am going through a serious dill phase these days and add it to everything. This is such a delicious combination; you must try it.

Heat 2½ tbsp of the oil in a large non-stick frying pan. Add the cumin seeds and, once they have browned a little, add the ginger and potatoes. Sauté for five minutes, then add the spices and some salt and stir well to coat. Cover and cook over a low flame for another seven or eight minutes, stirring every now and then.

Moving the potatoes to one side of the pan (and, if necessary, taking some out for a moment) tip the pan so that an empty edge is on the flame. Add the remaining oil into that space and, after it has had 10 seconds to heat up, add the garlic and cook for one minute or until it smells cooked. Stir it into the potatoes, returning any that you had taken out.

Cook for another couple of minutes, then add a splash of water to the pan, cover and cook until the potatoes are cooked through, another few minutes or so. Add the lemon juice and dill, taste, adjust the seasoning and serve.

Serves 4

3 tbsp vegetable oil
2 tsp cumin seeds
10g root ginger, peeled weight, finely shredded
450g potatoes, peeled and cut into 2–3cm pieces
½ tsp turmeric
⅛ tsp chilli powder
2 tsp ground coriander
½ tsp ground cumin
salt and freshly ground black pepper
4 fat garlic cloves, chopped
2–3 tsp lemon juice, or to taste
40g chopped dill fronds

Edgy peas

I do love peas. I love their yielding texture, sweetness and subtle flavour, plus I always have some in the freezer and as we all know they cook in minutes. But – and it is a big but – sometimes they can be a bit blah. I need *more* flavour... so this is what peas taste like when they venture out of their safe 'vanilla' zone! Use lemon juice if you don't have mango powder.

Heat the oil in a saucepan. Add the cumin seeds and, when they darken, add the ginger and cook until it colours. Stir in the coriander, garam masala and some salt.

Add the peas and fenugreek leaves and cook for a couple of minute so that any excess moisture dries up. Add the milk and cook over a moderate flame, stirring often, until the milk, too, has evaporated. Stir in the mango powder, taste and adjust the seasoning, adding lots of black pepper. Serve.

Serves 4

2 tbsp vegetable oil
1 rounded tsp cumin seeds
20g root ginger, peeled weight, finely shredded
2 tsp ground coriander
¾ tsp garam masala
salt and lots of fresh ground black pepper
400g frozen peas, defrosted
2 tsp dried fenugreek leaves
120ml whole milk
1–1½ tsp mango powder (*amchoor*), or to taste

Tamarind and chilli-glazed sweet potatoes

This is a brilliant combination of flavours: sticky sweet, spicy and tangy. Sweet potatoes are so healthy that I often make myself eat them, but I need lots of contrasting flavours to make their sweetness – cherished by others – palatable to me... *except* when I make this dish, which I find hard to stop eating. It makes a vibrant accompaniment to most dishes.

Heat the oil in a non-stick saucepan over a medium heat. Add the mustard seeds and chillies and cook until the popping starts to calm down. Add the lentils and curry leaves and, once the lentils start to colour, add the ginger and cook for 30–40 seconds. Stir in the tomato purée and cook for another minute or so.

Add the sweet potato and some salt, then pour in enough water to come three-quarters of the way up the potatoes. Bring to a boil, then cover and cook for 10–12 minutes, or until they start to soften.

Uncover, add the sugar and tamarind and stir well, cooking off the excess water and stirring the potatoes all the while. You should end up with a sticky glaze which has coated the potatoes. Taste and adjust the salt, tamarind and sugar to taste and serve.

Serves 3–4

3 tbsp vegetable oil
1 tsp mustard seeds
2–4 dried chillies
1 tbsp *urad dal* (skinned black gram)
10 fresh curry leaves
10g root ginger, peeled weight, finely chopped
2 tsp tomato purée
500g sweet potato (around 2 smallish), peeled and cut into 5cm chunks
salt
2 tsp caster sugar, or to taste
2 tsp tamarind paste, or to taste

Herby quinoa and chickpea salad

Inspired by tabbouleh, this lovely salad contrasts creamy quinoa with mealy chickpeas. It is healthy, flavourful and delicious. I like to serve it with a little goat's curd or cheese or feta crumbled over the top. This is a really versatile salad that I make often at home.

Boil the quinoa according to the packet instructions (usually a matter of about 15 minutes). Leave to cool a little. Meanwhile, prepare the rest of the ingredients.

Mix the quinoa with all the remaining ingredients, except the goat's curd or cheese (if using), taste and adjust the salt, sugar and lemon juice if necessary. Leave for 10 minutes to allow the flavours to come together. If using goat's curd, spoon dots over the salad, or crumble goat's cheese over it. Serve at room temperature.

Serves 4

70g quinoa
100g parsley leaves, finely chopped
30g mint leaves, finely chopped
3 spring onions, finely chopped
2 ripe tomatoes, finely chopped
1 small red chilli, deseeded and finely chopped (optional)
3 tsp roasted ground cumin (see page 92)
400g can of chickpeas, drained and rinsed
2½–3 tbsp extra virgin olive oil
3 tsp red wine vinegar
salt
1 tsp caster sugar, or to taste
2 tbsp lemon juice, or to taste
100g goat's curd or cheese (optional)

Cumin quinoa with smoked almonds

You can add some sliced and sautéed onions for a bit of sweetness, or raisins or other dried fruit, though this is great as a simple side dish as it is.

Dry-toast the quinoa in a large sauté pan over a medium heat until the grains smell toasted and have coloured a little. Add the stock or water and a good pinch of salt, bring to the boil, then simmer until the quinoa is cooked, about 15 minutes. As the water evaporates, give the pan a stir with a fork. The goal is to have fluffy grains, so if, when there is only two or three minutes to go, there seems to be a lot of water in the pan, increase the heat a bit. Once the quinoa is ready, turn up the heat and cook off any excess liquid if there is any, while stirring with a fork.

Meanwhile, heat the oil in a small pan, add the cumin seeds and, once they have toasted, stir into the quinoa with the almonds, herbs and salt to taste. Serve hot.

Serves 4

250g quinoa
800ml vegetable stock or water
salt
1 tbsp vegetable oil
1 tsp black cumin seeds (*shahi jeera*), or regular cumin seeds
handful of smoked almonds, halved
handful of chopped coriander or parsley leaves

Sticky tamarind-glazed aubergines

A lovely easy recipe inspired by the popular Japanese dish of aubergines with miso, except using my new favourite tamarind chutney, which you can buy or make at home (see page 155). The long, thin aubergines you can buy these days are perfect for this.

Preheat the oven to 200°C/400°F/gas mark 6. Heat the oil and fry the ginger shreds until golden. Strain the oil (reserve it) and place the ginger on kitchen paper.

Place the aubergines on an ovenproof baking tray, cut-side up. Score them in a criss-cross pattern, being careful not to go through the skin. Brush with the reserved ginger-flavoured oil and season lightly with salt. Place in the oven and bake for 15 minutes. Remove from the oven, turn it off, and preheat the grill.

Brush the aubergines with a thick coating of tamarind chutney, liberally sprinkle over the sesame seeds and place beneath the hot grill for three to four minutes or until bubbling. Serve sprinkled with the ginger.

Serve 4–6

2 tbsp olive oil

50g root ginger, peeled weight, finely shredded

12 baby aubergines, halved lengthways

salt

5–6 tbsp shop-bought tamarind and date chutney, or home-made (see page 155)

2 tbsp toasted sesame seeds (store bought or toasted in a dry pan for 1–2 minutes)

time-saving star: *shop-bought tamarind and date chutney*

Ultimate speedy kachumber

I make no apology for including this wonderful Indian chopped salad recipe, though I have published it before. It is the classic version, and my best recipe for it. A kachumber is served with many Indian meals; it is crunchy, fresh and delicious. I have omitted the green chillies that often go in. If you like their clean heat, add 1 small green chilli, deseeded and finely chopped. You can also add chopped mint leaves instead of dried if you prefer.

Mix everything together. Taste and adjust the seasoning and serve. That's it!

Serves 4–5, can be doubled

2 largish ripe tomatoes, chopped
200g cucumber, chopped
4 small radishes, trimmed, halved and finely chopped
$\frac{1}{3}$–$\frac{1}{2}$ small red onion, finely chopped
large handful of chopped coriander leaves
1 tbsp extra virgin olive oil
2 tbsp lemon juice, or to taste
1 tsp roasted ground cumin, or to taste (see page 92)
1 tbsp good-quality dried mint, crushed to a powder between your fingers
salt and a good pinch of freshly ground black pepper

Crunchy Indian slaw

This Indian version of coleslaw is crunchy, tangy, creamy and with the added zing of chaat masala. If you don't want to use two colours of cabbage, just one would be fine.

Squeeze out any juices from the shredded carrot. Place in a bowl and mix in the remaining ingredients. Taste and adjust the levels of lemon, chaat masala and seasoning until it tastes perfect to you. Take it to the table.

Serves 4

1 carrot (about 100g), finely sliced or coarsely grated
100g shredded red cabbage
100g shredded white cabbage
$\frac{1}{2}$ small red onion, finely sliced
large handful of chopped coriander leaves
70g mayonnaise (light is fine)
70g Greek yogurt
$1\frac{1}{2}$–2 tbsp lemon juice, to taste
$1\frac{1}{2}$ tsp chaat masala, or to taste
salt and freshly ground black pepper

Near-instant grilled naan

This is the quickest naan you will ever cook, it comes together in minutes, needs only a short knead, then cooks again in moments. On the table in less than 15 minutes.

Preheat the oven to its highest setting (mine goes up to 275°C/530°F). Place a grill shelf or baking sheet on the highest shelf to heat through.

Mix together all the dry ingredients. Make a well in the middle and add the wet ingredients, including the 20g of melted butter. Bring together into a dough, it should be quite soft; if not add more water. Knead quickly until smooth.

Roll out into ½cm-thick breads on a lightly floured surface. Pat in some nigella seeds, coriander leaves, or garlic – or nothing if you don't want a topping – and place in the hot oven. Cook two at a time until light spots or a light golden colour appear on the upper surface, then turn over and cook the underside for a minute or so. Take out, brush with butter and keep the breads warm by wrapping in a napkin or foil and placing in a warm place while you make the rest. Serve hot.

Makes 4 large breads

300g plain flour, plus more
  to dust
1⅓ tsp baking powder
½ tsp bicarbonate of soda
⅔ tsp salt
2 tsp caster sugar
4 tbsp milk
4 tbsp plain yogurt
90–100ml water
20g unsalted butter, melted,
  plus more to serve

Optional toppings
good couple of pinches
  of nigella seeds,
  or other seeds
chopped coriander leaves
finely chopped garlic

make it better: *roast your own poppadums*

I generally always cook my own poppadums (see page 128 for a photo), as I don't like the fried ones you buy in the shops. All Indian stores (real and online) will sell different varieties of these. To cook them you'll need an open flame and a pair of tongs. Take a poppadum in the tongs and place it over the flame, keeping it moving so that all bits of the poppadum are exposed to the direct flame, but no part actually burns. Once it is puffed up and crisp all over, it is done. They will only take one or two minutes each and you'll find they are a revelation.

Superfood Peshwari naan

Every time I make naan, I wonder why I don't do so more often. Peshwari naan comes from a region on the border of Afghanistan and Pakistan. It is close to the area where my mother grew up (then a part of India) and, as my grandfather brought nuts and dried fruits from Afghanistan to India, the family always had a bountiful supply. When my mother came to the UK, she continued to fill the house with both and I do the same now... clearly inherited habits. These naans are easy to make and as visually stunning as they are delicious, as well as being full of health-giving superfoods. They are also addictive...

Mix all the dry ingredients for the dough in a bowl. Make a well in the middle and add the wet ingredients (not the oil). Knead well for six to eight minutes, or until it is soft and springy. Grease the dough ball with a little oil and place back in the bowl, cover with a tea towel and plate and leave in a warmish or draft-free place for one hour.

Meanwhile, pound or blend together all the ingredients for the filling until it is a paste, adding a couple of spoons of water to help it break down (but it doesn't have to be smooth, so don't worry if it isn't).

Preheat the grill (and oven, if possible) to the highest setting and place your oven rack or baking tray on the upper shelf. Divide the dough into six balls and, taking one at a time, pat it out into a 7.5cm circle. Place 1 tbsp of the filling in the centre, bring the sides up and make into a pouch, pressing the edges in. Place on a floured surface, seam-side down and pat a little to make a thick flatbread, making sure the paste spreads out inside. Then roll out into a tear- or oval-shaped 1–1½cm-thick naan and prick with a fork. Repeat to make the remaining breads and place three at a time on the hot baking shelf.

Bake until the surface has some lovely golden spots, around three minutes, then flip and bake for another two or three minutes until the other side has also cooked through. Brush with butter and keep the breads warm by wrapping in a napkin or some foil and placing them in a warm place while you make the rest. Serve hot.

Makes 6 medium-large breads

For the dough
300g plain flour, plus more
   to dust
3 tsp caster sugar
1 tsp salt
1 tsp dried yeast
2 tbsp melted butter or ghee,
   plus more to brush
4 tbsp plain yogurt
150ml water
a little flavourless oil

For the filling
40g goji berries
40g cranberries
40g raisins
30g pine nuts
30g cashew nuts
30g ground almonds
1–2 tsp violet syrup or
   rose water
good pinch of ground fennel
   seeds (optional)

Roti

The basic, everyday wholewheat flatbread many Indians eat with their meals, roti (also known as chapati) adds a chewy, nutty element to a meal. You can find chapati flour (*atta*) in most large supermarkets, but, if you can't get any, use equal quantities of wholewheat and plain flour. Roti can be made in advance and reheated, wrapped in foil, in a medium oven.

Makes 10 breads

300g chapati flour (*atta*), plus more to dust
salt (optional)
200–240ml water

Sift the flour and some salt (if using) into a bowl and make a well in the centre. Slowly drizzle in most of the water and, using your hand, draw the flour into the centre, mixing all the time. You may not need all the water, as flour absorbs different amounts depending on its age and the moisture content in the air. The dough should be just slightly sticky and almost squeak as you knead, but will firm up as you work it.

Knead for eight to 10 minutes, or until the dough seems elastic. Place in a bowl, cover with a damp tea towel and leave for 30 minutes if you have the time.

Divide the dough into 10 portions and roll into golf ball-sized balls, then cover. Flour your work surface and rolling pin. Roll each ball into 12.5–15cm diameter circles. The best way to do this is to keep rolling in one direction, giving the dough quarter-turns to get a round shape.

Heat a tava (an Indian flat griddle pan) or a non-stick frying pan until quite hot. Toss the roti from one hand to the other to remove excess flour, then place on the tava. Reduce the heat to medium, cook until small bubbles appear underneath, 10–20 seconds, then flip. Cook this side until it has small, dark beige spots.

The best way to puff a roti is to place it directly over an open flame (with the brown spotted side on the top), using tongs. It will puff immediately. Cook it for 10 seconds until dark spots appear; I like to move it around the flame for even puffing. Place on a plate. Repeat with the rest. If you only have an electric cooker, press down gently on the cooked roti over the heat; as you press one area the rest should puff up. Then tackle the next area. This way the roti should puff up all over.

Keep the bread warm by wrapping in a napkin or some foil and keeping it in a low oven while you make the rest.

Paratha, three ways

If these flaky, slightly crisp flatbreads are a favourite of yours, you'll be delighted to know you can prepare and cook them in minutes. There is a knack to them, but you will pick it up very quickly. My two favourite flavoured parathas are here, but you can add anything you like.

Mix the water into the flour and knead until you have a smooth dough. Make a long log from the dough, then divide it into 10 balls. Cover.

Heat a tava (an Indian flat griddle pan) or a non-stick frying pan. Taking one ball of dough at a time, roll it out into 15cm circle, using a little extra flour. Spread ¾ tsp of the oil, ghee or butter over the surface, sprinkle over a little salt and a fine scattering of the flour, plus any flavourings you want to use (or simply leave them plain). Starting with the far edge of the bread, roll towards you into a very tight log (Swiss-roll style), then use your palms to roll this log a bit longer and thinner. Coil the log on itself in a tight circle and pat down into a thick disc. Flour both sides and roll out into a 15–17.5cm circle again.

Pat off the excess flour and place on the hot pan, increasing the heat to medium-high. Cook until light brown spots appear on the underside, around 10–15 seconds. Turn over and spread ¾ tsp more oil, ghee or butter over the surface. (I spread it with the back of a spoon.) Flip the bread again and repeat with more oil. Also, using the edge of the spoon or a knife, make small slashes over the bread (this will help it crisp up). Turn once again and repeat the slashes. By now the bread should be done, with some lovely golden brown spots on both sides.

Keep the bread warm by wrapping in a napkin or some foil and keeping it in a low oven while you make the rest. Serve hot or at room temperature.

Makes 10 breads

200–220ml water
300g chapati flour (*atta*), plus
  more to dust
small bowl of vegetable oil,
  ghee or melted butter
good pinch of salt

For the flavour variations

spicy
sprinkle a pinch each of carom seeds and chilli powder over each bread with the salt, then flour, roll and cook as in the main recipe

mint
sprinkle ¾ tsp dried mint (powdered between your finger) over each bread with the salt, then flour, roll and cook as in the main recipe

Grilled marinated vegetables

In India, there was always a plate of sliced salad vegetables on the table when we went to friends' homes for dinner. The platter normally consisted of sliced cucumber, mooli (Indian radish and its leaves) and carrots that were simply dressed with lemon juice, salt and chilli powder. They were always refreshing. This is an updated version of those memories, the charring works really well with Indian meals and there is still crunch. If you don't want to grill the vegetables, you can just finely slice them all and toss them in the dressing.

Heat a griddle pan or preheat a grill on its highest setting. If using a griddle, add the fennel and cook it undisturbed until it has nice char lines, then turn and do the same on the other side. Set aside and repeat with the asparagus and courgette. If using a grill, place the rack on the highest level and cook the asparagus first, as it cooks the quickest and is a bit fiddly. Grill for a few minutes or until charred on the edges. Place in a bowl. Repeat with the fennel and courgette.

Meanwhile, stir together the ingredients for the dressing (omit the coriander if you have radish leaves), taste and adjust the seasoning.

Once all the vegetables have been griddled or grilled, toss them in the dressing with the radishes and their leaves (if using) and serve.

Serves 3–4

For the vegetables
1 large fennel bulb, any tough
  outer layers removed, trimmed
  and finely sliced
12 asparagus spears, trimmed
  and finely sliced on the diagonal
1 large courgette, finely sliced
  on the diagonal
4–5 radishes with leaves if
  possible, leaves shredded
  and radishes finely sliced

For the dressing
4 tbsp extra virgin olive oil
2 tsp red wine or sherry vinegar
5 tsp lemon juice
4 tbsp chopped coriander
  leaves and stalks (optional,
  omit if you have radish leaves)
1/4 tsp chilli powder
pinch of caster sugar
salt and freshly ground
  black pepper

Southern carrot and peanut raita

An Indian west coast-style raita that is nutty, creamy, crunchy and lightly sweetened.

Mix the carrots, yogurt, salt, pepper, sugar, half the coriander and all the peanuts.

Heat the oil in a small saucepan, allowing the liquid to pool on one side. Add the mustard seeds and, when the popping starts to die down, add the curry leaves and cook for another 10 seconds or so. Stir into the yogurt and serve garnished with the remaining coriander.

Serves 4

2 large carrots, finely sliced or
  coarsely grated, water
  squeezed out
400g plain yogurt
salt and freshly ground
  black pepper
1½ tsp caster sugar, or to taste
3 tbsp chopped
  coriander leaves
20g roasted peanuts,
  lightly crushed
1 tsp olive oil
¾ tsp mustard seeds
6–7 fresh curry leaves

Cucumber and mint raita

A refreshing raita that is really versatile, great with grilled meats or just with some naan or pitta bread.

Squeeze all the excess water from the cucumber and place it in a large bowl. Add the remaining ingredients and stir well. Chill until ready to serve.

Serves 3–4

200g cucumber (½ large),
  coarsely grated
400g thick plain yogurt
salt and freshly ground
  black pepper
8g mint leaves, shredded
¾ tsp roasted ground cumin
  (see page 92)
small pinch of caster sugar

Tomato, onion and cucumber raita

This is my favourite raita and the one we eat most often at home.

Stir all the ingredients together and season to taste. That's it!

Serves 4

1 small vine tomato, chopped
  into 1cm dice
90g cucumber, peeled and
  chopped into 1cm dice
¼ red onion, finely chopped
large handful of chopped
  coriander leaves
¾ tsp roasted ground cumin
  (see page 92)
400g plain yogurt
salt and freshly ground
  black pepper

Coastal coconut chutney

This is a really lovely chutney from the South of India and adds a wonderfully creamy coconut flavour to any meal or starter.

Dry-roast the chana dal until it has coloured all over but has not gone brown. Add to the coconut in a bowl with the chilli, ginger, some salt, most of the lemon juice and 3–4 tbsp of water. Blend until everything has broken down (I use a hand-held blender). You may need to add 1 tbsp of the yogurt to assist the blending process.

Heat the oil in a small saucepan, letting it pool on one side. Add the mustard seeds and, once the popping dies down, add the curry leaves and cook for another 10 seconds. Pour into the chutney with the remaining yogurt. Stir it all together, taste and adjust the salt and lemon juice.

Makes about 175ml

3 tbsp *chana dal* (Bengal gram)
100g finely grated fresh
  coconut, fresh or frozen
  and defrosted
1 green chilli
8g root ginger, peeled weight,
  coarsely chopped
salt
1 tbsp lemon juice, or to taste
3 tbsp Greek yogurt
1 tsp vegetable oil
$\frac{2}{3}$ tsp mustard seeds
8 fresh curry leaves

Tangy coriander chutney

This is the chutney that I use the most. It is tangy, herby and very fresh. It goes with snacks and street food, in sandwiches, marinades and with almost anything, adding a sense of vibrancy wherever it appears.

Whizz everything together with 2½–3 tbsp of water until very smooth and homogenous. Taste and adjust the salt and lemon juice to taste.

Makes 200ml

50g coriander leaves and stalks
20g mint leaves
$2\frac{1}{4}$–$2\frac{1}{2}$ tbsp lemon juice,
  or to taste
30g roasted shelled pistachios
$\frac{1}{2}$–1 green chilli
salt

make it easier: *frozen chutney*

I often whizz together a big batch of this and freeze it in a shallow container; it is easy to scrape some from the top when I need it, or use a knife to cut out a frozen block and ease it out of the container.

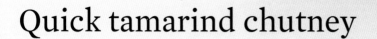

Quick tamarind chutney

This is a really quick and easy version of the tamarind and date chutney that is used in India almost as ketchup is used in the West, as a sweet, tangy and lightly spicy condiment to perk up any dish. The tartness of tamarind is balanced by the sweetness of jaggery and the simple spices add a wonderful flavour. I am a big fan of jaggery; it has a caramel flavour that mimics the taste normally given by dates to this chutney, and it is completely unrefined. It is not so difficult to find, but you can use a brown sugar instead if you can't get it.

Put everything in a small saucepan with 80ml of water, bring to the boil and simmer for four to five minutes or until it has thickened and is lightly syrupy. It will continue to thicken once cool.

Cool and serve, or keep in the fridge (it will be fine there for a couple of weeks).

Enough to serve with snacks for 4 people

2½ good tsp tamarind paste
40–50g jaggery, chopped up, or muscovado sugar
1 tsp roasted ground cumin (see page 92)
¼ tsp freshly ground black pepper
¼ tsp salt

Mint and garlic yogurt

I gave this recipe before in *I Love Curry*, but I love it and eat it all the time, so here it is again!

Mix all the ingredients together, taste, adjust the seasoning and serve.

Serves 4–5

400g full- or half-fat Greek yogurt
1 garlic clove, grated
10 large mint leaves, shredded
salt

SHORT AND SWEET

Pomegranate poached rhubarb with spiced biscuits

An easy but impressive dessert that makes the most of rhubarb when the pinkest batons come into season during late winter. Rhubarb works really well with pomegranate and tangerine and the spices here add a lovely warmth. The simple biscuits are crunchy, buttery and so moreish that the recipe makes more than you need, so you can munch on them for days after the dessert is a sweet memory… and they can be made a few days in advance.

First make the biscuits: preheat the oven to 180°C/350°F/gas mark 4 and line a baking tray with baking parchment. Cream the butter and sugar together until light and fluffy. Add the spices and salt and sift in the flours. Gently mix together but do not overwork. Still working gently, make roughly walnut-sized balls of dough; there should be 12–14. Flatten each gently until about ¾cm thick and carefully place on the baking tray, spaced well apart as they will spread.

Bake in the hot oven for 22–24 minutes, or until turning golden at the edges. Remove and cool on the baking tray, then transfer to a wire rack with a palette knife. Be careful, as they are quite fragile. When completely cold, store in an airtight tin; they will be fine for up to a week.

Now for the fruit. Place the two juices, the zest, cinnamon or cassia and sugar in a saucepan and bring to the boil. Simmer for five minutes, then add the rhubarb and simmer for another five to seven minutes, depending on thickness. The outer bits will start to look soft (they will continue to cook). Remove the rhubarb from the liquor with a slotted spoon and place on a plate. Reduce the juices for another four or five minutes, or until very lightly syrupy.

Serve the rhubarb with some of the juices spooned over and a sprinkling of pistachios (if using). Add a dollop of thick Greek yogurt or crème fraîche and a couple of biscuits.

Serves 4

For the spiced biscuits (makes 12–14)
120g unsalted butter, at room temperature
80g light muscovado or soft brown sugar
½ tsp ground cardamom
1 tsp ground cinnamon
good pinch of salt
120g plain flour
60g cornflour

For the fruit
500ml pomegranate juice
juice and finely grated zest of 2 tangerines or clementines
20g cinnamon sticks or shards of cassia bark
100g caster sugar
450g early pink rhubarb, cut into 7.5cm batons
thick Greek yogurt or crème fraîche, to serve
chopped pistachios, to serve (optional)

Glazed pineapple with salted peanuts and coconut ice cream

I think pineapple is at its best when it is caramelised and, when paired with salted roast peanuts and cold coconut ice cream, it is paradise. For convenience, you can caramelise the pineapple earlier in the day and reheat it to serve. For an even easier version, cut the pineapple into large chunks instead of slicing it thin. Also, don't worry at all if the pieces are not all the same, it will look fine in the end.

You will need to caramelise the pineapple in three batches. Add 2 tbsp sugar per batch to the pan, place over a medium-low heat and allow to melt until it is a lovely golden caramel; do not stir. Add 4 tbsp of boiling water, swirl and, as the mixture bubbles, add one-third of the pineapple slices; they can overlap slightly. Cook, keeping them apart, and start turning them in the syrupy liquid until it reduces and thickens. Add one-third each of the butter and peanuts and continue. When the batch is finished, the caramel should be slightly thick and the pineapple glazed and golden on both sides. Repeat with the remaining two batches of pineapple, reheating them all gently together at the end.

Place the pineapple on warm plates, making sure you have evenly distributed the peanuts and caramel. Serve hot, with a small scoop of ice cream on each plate.

Serves 4

½–⅔ large pineapple, skinned and sliced as thinly as you can (about 20 thin slices)
6 tbsp caster sugar
30g unsalted butter
45g salted roast peanuts, roughly chopped
4 small scoops of good-quality coconut ice cream

make it better: *preparing pineapples*

Because pineapples have so many 'eyes', it can be a job to prepare them. Cut off all the skin with a heavy knife, then go back across the surface with a smaller, pointed knife, removing all the eyes with a gouging motion. When you come to slice the fruits, you will realise that not all pineapples are created equal. Some are so perfectly succulent that the core is tender and pleasant to eat; others have cores as tough and fibrous as old shoe leather. Take a view of your pineapple and discard the core if it is not good to eat.

Ginger chai tiramisu

For me, my daily drink of ginger chai is reviving, soothing and relaxing all at the same time. So combining my personal pick-me-up with the Italian classic, replacing the coffee with Indian tea, makes complete sense to me. This pudding is creamy and smooth with an underlying taste of cardamom and tea and an added zing from the ginger. I like to layer it up in individual glasses, just because it looks prettier.

To make the tea liquor, heat the milk in a saucepan with 180ml of water, add the spices and simmer on the lowest possible heat for six to eight minutes. Add the tea and cook for three to five minutes, until it is a rich colour. Leave to cool.

For the mascarpone cream, whisk the yolks with 1 tbsp of the sugar until smooth and pale. Add the mascarpone and ginger and whisk until smooth. Separately, whisk the egg white with the remaining sugar until it holds its shape. Spoon this over the mascarpone mixture, but do not mix it in. In a clean bowl, whip the cream to soft, billowing peaks. Spoon it on to the whites, add the liqueur (if using) and gently fold the whole thing together until smooth.

Strain the chai into a shallow dish. Dip the biscuits, one by one, into the tea for one or two seconds per side. Place into serving glasses, lining the bases. Top with a generous layer of mascarpone cream. Repeat the layers, then cover each glass and place in the fridge to chill for at least one hour and up to a day.

Finely grate over a layer of chocolate just before serving.

Serves 4–5, can be doubled

For the tea liquor
240ml whole milk
1 tsp black peppercorns
¼ tsp ground cardamom
5cm cinnamon stick
10g root ginger, peeled
  weight, grated
1½ tsp loose-leaf black tea,
  or 4 tea bags

For the mascarpone cream
2 egg yolks, plus 1 egg white
2 tbsp caster sugar
250g mascarpone
15g root ginger, peeled
  weight, grated
100ml double cream
1 tbsp ginger liqueur or dark
  rum (optional)

To assemble the tiramisu
100g savoiardi biscuits
30g good-quality dark chocolate
  (I recommend Lindt Chilli
  chocolate, it is fantastic!)

Near-instant berry, violet and star anise Eton mess

One of my summertime favourites. Indians use a lot of floral essences in their desserts and, having discovered this violet syrup, I find myself using it often. But you can substitute 1–2 tsp of rose essence mixed with icing sugar to taste, if you prefer a rose flavour. For the berries, I like to use sliced strawberries, raspberries and blueberries during the summer, then blackberries later in the year. Blackberry and violet is an amazing flavour combination. If you want to lighten the taste slightly, try adding 2 tbsp of Greek yogurt to the cream mixture.

Blend together one-third of the berries with the lemon juice and violet syrup to taste; you'll need to balance the amounts of sharp lemon juice and sweet syrup according to the tartness of the berries and the strength of the syrup. If you are going to be adding yogurt or sour cherries, remember that both of these will make the mixture more tart.

Lightly whip the cream so that it just holds its shape but is billowing and soft, then stir in the star anise, adding the yogurt and sour cherries if you want.

When you are ready to serve, place the meringues in a lage mixing bowl, top with the whole berries and the spiced cream and gently fold them all together. Drizzle over the scented fruit purée and fold once; it should be rippled rather than even. Spoon into a serving dish or individual glasses, top with the almonds and serve.

Serves 4–5, can be doubled

450g mixed berries
2 tsp lemon juice, to taste
4–5 tbsp violet syrup, to taste
350ml chilled double cream
1 large star anise, ground,
   or 1 tsp ground star anise
2 tbsp Greek yogurt (optional)
2 tbsp dried sour cherries
   (optional)
80g (3 medium-large nests)
   meringue, broken into
   medium-sized pieces
sprinkle of lightly toasted
   flaked almonds

10 mins to cook

Cheat's rasmalai

Rasmalai is definitely my favourite Indian dessert. In its authentic form it is made from spongy balls of paneer that have been cooked and soaked in sugar syrup, then placed into a fragrant, milky liquor. I have never made 'proper' rasmalai at home, as cooking the balls is an art form... and one I haven't taken the time to master. So when a Twitter follower, Mandeep Obhi, insisted it was really easy to cheat with ricotta, I had to give it a try. She was right. This is super-easy and really hits the spot. I have shortened the cooking time by using a small can of evaporated milk, but, if you prefer to use only whole milk, add another 400ml milk to the quantity below and reduce the volume of the milk liquor to about 500ml before chilling.

Make the milk liquor first. Bring the whole milk and ground cardamom to the boil in a very wide saucepan and reduce to just under half its quantity. If you do this over a medium-high heat, it should take around 20 minutes. Stir the milk every two or three minutes, making sure you scrape the base of the pan so the milk does not stick and burn. Any skin that forms on the surface should be stirred back in.

Add the sugar, evaporated milk and saffron and return to the boil. Simmer for two or three minutes, then take off the heat and stir in 40g of the ricotta. Cool, then chill in the fridge. (This can be done the day before serving.)

To make the ricotta balls, preheat the oven to 170°C/340°F/gas mark 3½. Mix the remaining 360g of ricotta with the icing sugar and spoon it into 12 mini muffin moulds. Bake for 20–40 minutes (fresh ricotta contains less water and cooks more quickly; long-life ricotta will take longer), or until the balls are springy when lightly pressed and can easily be removed from the tin. Remove from the oven. Cool, then place in the chilled milk liquor, cover and leave in the fridge for up to two days.

Serve the ricotta balls with some of their milky liquor, sprinkling with the pistachios to serve.

Serves 4

For the milk liquor
1 litre whole milk
½ tsp ground cardamom, or to taste
2 tbsp caster sugar, or to taste
150ml evaporated milk
good pinch of saffron strands

For the ricotta balls
400g ricotta, fresh is always best
35g icing sugar
3 tbsp pistachios, left whole if small, or halved or roughly chopped if large

Speedy saffron yogurt with cape gooseberries

The Indian dessert shrikand is a fantastic amalgam of thick creamy yogurt, musky saffron and aromatic green cardamom, with nuts added for texture. I have added cape gooseberries – also known as physalis – to the mix, and they add a delicious fruity freshness to the already beautiful pudding. Yogurt will vary in tartness, so add icing sugar to taste. For extra richness, you can fold in 100ml of softly whipped cream as well, if you like. I love desserts to be easy, but I do like to add a little whimsy. Here I garnish the dish with some white chocolate-covered physalis and sprinkle over some popping candy once they are almost dry. Guests don't see it coming and it is a childish sensation I don't seem to tire of...

Heat the milk, add the saffron and leave to infuse for 10–15 minutes, helping it along by pressing down with a spoon. You should have a nice, deep ochre colour.

Sift the icing sugar and ground cardamom into the yogurt and add the saffron milk and most of the nuts. Stir well, then cover and chill until ready to serve. When you're ready to eat, stir the sliced cape gooseberries into the yogurt mixture and spoon into individual glass dishes.

For a simple finish, serve sprinkled with the remaining almonds and some whole physalis (pull their jackets back so they 'fly in the air').

For a more light-hearted result, melt the white chocolate. (The quickest way is microwaved in a microwave-safe bowl for about 50 seconds.) Give it a stir, it should be have melted, if not heat for another 15–20 seconds. Dip the extra cape gooseberries (whose jackets have been pulled back) into the chocolate and place on an oiled plate, ideally chocolate-side up. After an hour or so, sprinkle over the popping candy. Serve the yogurt sprinkled with the remaining almonds and with the white-chocolate popping candy cape gooseberries arranged on top and watch your guests' faces light up!

Serves 4

1½ tbsp milk
½ tsp saffron strands
6–7 tbsp icing sugar, or to taste
¼ tsp freshly ground cardamom seeds, or to taste
600g Greek yogurt
3 tbsp flaked almonds, lightly toasted
200g cape gooseberries (sometimes sold as physalis), halved or quartered, plus more to serve
50g white chocolate (optional)
vegetable oil, (optional)
1 packet of popping candy (optional, see recipe introduction)

10 mins to cook

My quick-to-make almond cake

One of the Indian sweets my mother-in-law never fails to bring with her on visits to see us in London are almond *katlis*, made only with sugar and almond paste. They are very similar to marzipan, but without the egg whites. I discovered the original version of the recipe that follows in a magazine more than 10 years ago, adapted it to suit my tastes and it is now one of my family's favourites. It has the delicious almond flavour that we love and, most importantly, is best made a day or two earlier... so that you can make it when you have time, to eat when you're busy. It is crumbly, almondy and very moist and a little goes a long way. Lovely with a cup of tea, or as dessert with fruits and crème fraîche.

Preheat the oven to 180°C/350°F/gas mark 4. Lightly butter a 20cm cake tin and line the base with baking parchment.

Break the marzipan into small pieces and lightly beat it with an electric whisk to soften. Add the butter and sugar and continue whisking until creamy; it is important that the marzipan breaks down. Add the eggs one at a time, whisking between each addition. You may need to add 1 tbsp or so of flour towards the end to stop the mixture from curdling. Stir in the vanilla.

Fold in the remaining flour, baking powder, salt and ground almonds. Pour into the cake tin and bake in the oven for 50–60 minutes, or until a cocktail stick inserted into the centre comes out clean. It will be quite brown by the end, so cover the top with foil to stop it darkening further once it is golden, if you like.

Take the cake out of the oven and leave it to cool for 10–15 minutes. Turn it out of the tin and serve, or wrap it in foil and store in an airtight container where it will soften and improve for up to two days. Serve cold or warm, as you prefer.

Serves 8–10

200g unsalted butter, at room temperature, plus more for the tin
100g marzipan, at room temperature
120g caster sugar
3 large eggs
100g self-raising flour, sifted
½ tsp vanilla extract
½ tsp baking powder
pinch of salt
200g ground almonds

Yogurt and orange flower pannacotta with roast star anise plums

Yogurt is one of North India's favourite ingredients and its creaminess and slight tartness works so well in cleansing the palate after a meal. I have added only a slight fragrance to the pannacotta, as the plums provide a sweet, fruity, spiced counterpoint.

Soak the gelatine leaves in cold water.

Heat the cream, sugar and orange zest in a saucepan until the sugar has dissolved. Take off the heat and stir in the gelatine. Once it has dissolved, stir in the yogurt and orange flower water.

Divide between six x 150–200ml ramekins or pudding basins, or glasses (no need to line or oil them). Cover with cling film and chill in the fridge for at least four hours, or up to two days, until ready to eat.

For the plums, preheat the oven to 200°C/400°F/gas mark 6. Place all the plums in an ovenproof dish in which they fit snugly. Pour over the orange juice, tuck the star anise between the plums and sprinkle over the sugar. Roast in the oven for 30 minutes, or until the plums are soft (the time this takes will depend on the ripeness of the fruit). Leave the plums to cool a little in the sauce, turning them cut-side down so that they soak up some of the flavours and colours.

When you are ready to serve, either take the pannacottas to the table in the containers you set them in, or turn them out. To turn them out, dip the base of a pannacotta mould in boiling water for a few seconds, cover with a serving plate and invert to turn out. Repeat with the rest.

Serve with the plums, cut into wedges if you like, spooning their spiced liquor over the fruits.

Makes 6

For the pannacotta
4½ leaves of gelatine
320ml double cream
120g caster sugar
finely grated zest of 1 orange
  (use the juice in the plums)
400ml plain full-fat yogurt
1½ tsp orange flower water

For the star anise plums
6 plums, halved and pitted
180ml freshly squeezed orange
  juice (2–3 oranges)
6 star anise
4 tbsp caster sugar, or to taste

Indian brioche pudding with mangoes

Indians have a popular pudding called *shahi tukra*. It is a rich, special occasion dessert that takes hours to make, so this is my easy update. In fact, I think I prefer it to the authentic recipe. I use mangoes here, but you can use any ripe, soft fruit that is in season. You can toast and caramelise the bread in advance – and even scoop the ice cream into portions and return it to the freezer – so all you have to do on the evening is assemble the pudding.

Cut the brioche loaf into 12 slices. I like to cut the slices into circles, using my largest biscuit cutter, which is just shy of 10cm (though this is merely for presentation; leave the slices whole if you prefer).

Take four of the slices and split them very carefully horizontally with a serrated knife, to create eight thin slices.

Toast all the brioche slices, fatter and thinner, in a toaster or a large frying pan – pressing down with a fish slice or a broad spatula – so that they are golden and crisp on both sides. Set aside.

Pour the sugar into the frying pan and place over a low heat. Melt the sugar gently and allow it to caramelise; do not stir. Reduce the heat to the lowest possible setting. Using just the thin brioche slices, carefully but quickly dip one side into the caramel so that it has a light coating (I use forks or tongs). Place straight on to a baking tray, glazed-side up. Repeat with the remaining thin slices, turning the heat off from under the pan if the caramel is becoming too dark.

Around 15 minutes before you want to eat, scoop out eight balls of ice cream. Place in a large bowl and add the crème fraîche and ground cardamom. Encourage the ice cream to start to melt on the edges and mix it with the cream and spice.

Place a thick brioche slice on each of eight serving plates and scoop over one-eighth of the ice cream mixture with any remaining cream in the bowl. Scatter the mango slices over the top, sprinkle with the nuts and top each at an angle with a slice of the thin, caramel-dipped brioche. Give the puddings another few minutes so that the ice cream starts to melt into the thick slice of brioche, then serve.

Serves 8 (but scale up to make as many as you need)

1 brioche loaf
100g caster sugar
320g good-quality clotted cream ice cream, or other unflavoured ice cream
8 tbsp crème fraîche (half-fat if you prefer)
good pinch of ground cardamom
4 ripe, sweet mangoes, sliced
toasted flaked almonds, or pistachios, to serve

Coconut soufflé

Soufflés have a scary reputation but are actually not so hard to make, and they are about the most impressive desserts you can bring to the table. These soufflés are a great way of finishing a meal; they rise a mile and get very sophisticated when paired, as here, with a creamy, bitter coffee ice cream. Together the flavours are the essence of South India. You can also pair the soufflé with chocolate- or fruit-flavoured ice creams, or serve them just as they are.

Preheat the oven to 190°C/375°F/gas mark 5.

Put the coconut milk, butter, the 70g of desiccated coconut and 30g of the sugar into a saucepan. Place over a medium heat and bring to a boil, then cook for a few minutes, stirring all the time.

Meanwhile, stir 2 tbsp of cold water into the cornflour until smooth. Add this to the pan and return to the boil, stirring. Reduce the heat and simmer gently for five to seven minutes, or until the coconut mixture is thick. Leave to cool.

Place the egg whites in a food mixer and whisk until they hold soft peaks. Add the remaining 30g of sugar and whisk until the peaks are firm and glossy.

Quickly dry-toast the 25g of desiccated coconut in a small dry frying pan until golden, watching carefully so that it does not catch and burn. Butter six x 150ml ramekins and spoon in the toasted coconut, tipping the ramekins to coat all sides. Tip out the excess.

Stir one-quarter of the egg whites into the cooled coconut mix. Then add the coconut mix to the remaining egg whites and – really gently – fold the whole thing together with a large metal spoon.

Spoon the mixture into the prepared ramekins and level the surface with a palette knife. Run your thumb around the inner edge of each, making a small shallow indentation all the way round, then place on a baking tray and swiftly put into the hot oven, shutting the door quickly but gently.

Cook for 16–18 minutes, or until well risen and golden on the top. The soufflés will rise before this time, but need the extra few minutes to cook through. Do not open the oven door to check on them earlier, or they may sink.

Remove from the oven, place on plates and serve immediately with a small scoop of coffee ice cream and a dusting of cinnamon.

Makes 6

375ml creamy coconut milk
3 rounded tsp salted butter,
  plus more for the ramekins
70g desiccated coconut, plus
  25g more for the ramekins
60g caster sugar
5 level tsp cornflour
3 large egg whites
good-quality coffee ice cream,
  to serve
a little ground cinnamon,
  to serve

ACKNOWLEDGEMENTS

I often feel that being a working mum is one of the more difficult roles one can have and that sometimes one struggles to put 100 per cent into anything. But the team who helped me put this book together, many of whom are parents themselves, made it much easier... and make it look easy, too.

Thank you, Anne, for commissioning this book, which I have absolutely loved writing, as well as for your continued belief in me. Also to the team at Quadrille, for your consistent support with this and my other books. It is really appreciated and I know I don't say it enough.

Thank you to Heather and Claire, as always, for being so great, for having your finger on the pulse and trying to steer me in the right direction.

Thank you, Sam, for all your help, being my first proper sounding board in the kitchen. This book would never have been as 'amazzing' without you.

Lucy B, thank you for being so thorough and generally brilliant with words; the book reads so much better because of it. Lucy G, thank you for making the book look so beautiful and for listening to all my crazy design ideas and even incorporating a few of them. Lisa, I love your never-say-die attitude and the food looks even better because of it, thank you. Tabitha, the publishing world is a more beautiful place with you in it, thank you. Joss, you are such a star, cooking without breaks, making every dish look so delicious and being so much fun on the shoots.

Thank you to all of my extended family for being so understanding when I forget to do things I should be doing, and for never letting the hibernating me feel lonely. To my little monkeys/tiddlywinks, I love you more than you will ever know and my world is so much more fun and colourful with you in it.

Anjum Anand is on a mission to bring Indian food up to date. Very health-conscious herself, she is constantly working to create lighter dishes with all the rich flavours of the subcontinent. Anjum grew up in London, has presented two successful series of BBC TV's *Indian Food Made Easy* and written five best-selling books, all published by Quadrille. She has lived and studied in Geneva, Paris and Madrid and worked in restaurants in New York, Los Angeles and New Delhi, but her real love is home-cooked Indian food. Anjum travels regularly to India, but lives in London with her husband and two children. She has developed an internationally successful range of Indian sauces, chutneys and pickles, The Spice Tailor.

ALSO BY ANJUM ANAND:
Anjum's Indian Vegetarian Feast
I Love Curry
Anjum's Eat Right for Your Body Type
Anjum's New Indian
Indian Food Made Easy
Anjum's Quick & Easy Indian, *Anjum's Indian Vegetarian Feast* and *I Love Curry* are also available as eBooks on the iBook store.